THE OTHER SIDE OF LIFE

CONTENTS

		Page
INTRODUCTION		7
CHAPTER 1	**DONYATT**	9
CHAPTER 2	**RIDING AT DENFORD**	13
CHAPTER 3	**LONDON**	21
CHAPTER 4	**HOLIDAY IN SCOTLAND**	25
CHAPTER 5	**ISLE OF WIGHT**	27
CHAPTER 6	**WALKING BULLS AND RIDING ARAB STALLIONS**	31
CHAPTER 7	**SCHOOL DAYS - NEW HALL**	35
CHAPTER 8	**BLAINSLIE**	41
CHAPTER 9	**DAY SCHOOL-DUNS**	45
CHAPTER 10	**GIRL GROOM**	51
CHAPTER 11	**HOLIDAYS IN THE LAKE DISTRICT**	55
CHAPTER 12	**CONNAUGHT SQUARE**	59
CHAPTER 13	**CAUGHT BY THE TIDE**	63
CHAPTER 14	**STUDENT YEARS**	65
CHAPTER 15	**CAMBRIDGE**	69
CHAPTER 16	**THE ROYAL CALEDONIAN BAL**	71
CHAPTER 17	**BLAKENEY**	75
CHAPTER 18	**I LEARNED TO DRIVE**	79
CHAPTER 19	**CALAMATIES**	81
CHAPTER 20	**HORSES AND COACHES**	85
CHAPTER 21	**ITALIAN HOLIDAY**	89
CHAPTER 22	**FRENCH HOLIDAY**	93
CHAPTER 23	**COMING OUT**	97
CHAPTER 24	**PRINCESS MUSBAH**	101
CHAPTER 25	**FRANCES' WEDDING**	105
CHAPTER 26	**MUSIC**	107
CHAPTER 27	**LIVING WITH UNCLE ARTHUR AND AUNT GEORGINA**	109
CHAPTER 28	**I QUALIFY**	113

CHAPTER SOURCES

Introduction	John Spencer Churchill "Crowded Canvas. Memoirs of JSC" Odham Press 1961
Chapter 1	Peter Morley-Fletcher "The Allies in Italy 1943-1946. A translation of a British Officer's Selected Personal War-time Memorabilia" 2003
Chapter 2	Tony Tuckwell "New Hall and its School" Free Range Publishing 2006
Chapter 4	Katherine Duchess of Athol "Working Partnership" Arthur Baker Ltd 1958
Chapter 7	Tony Tuckwell "New Hall and its School" 2006 "Palace of Beaulieu" New Hall website
Chapter 10	Sally Connolly-Carew "The Children of Castletown" History Press Ireland 2012
Chapter 24	HRH Pincess Musbah Haidar "Arabesque" Hutchinsons & Co 1948
Chapter 26	Sheridan Russell "Sheridan's Story" William Barnes 1993

INTRODUCTION

In 1947, when I was five years old, my mother, Lady Daphne Fletcher, nee Hay, Hugo, my elder brother, and I, left Yester at Gifford. This was the large house belonging to my grandfather, the Eleventh Marquis of Tweeddale, where we had been living an idealistic life during the war, together with sixteen children, four nannies, three aunts, one great aunt, various refugees, and several step relations. Our grandmother, Midge Tweeddale, had died at the age of 47 years when I was two years old and had been replaced by our step-grandmother, Marjorie Nettlefold and her relations. (See The Children of Yester).

"Aunt" Marjorie's brother, Kenneth Wagg, then married to Catherine Horlicks, was Managing Director of Horlicks, the milk drink company, and owned a farm, Donyatt in Somerset, to which we were going. The plan was to run the farm, consisting of battery hens and pigs, which were to be fed on waste products from the Horlicks factory in Slough. Sir James Horlicks, Kenneth's father-in-law, owned the island of Gigha, which had a very famous garden. As well as the battery hens, we had our own free range hens which were very tame and we treated them as pets.

We were accompanied by Sally Churchill, Winston Churchill's great niece, now Lady Ashburton. She had been with us at Yester for most of

THE OTHER SIDE OF LIFE

the war, although her father, Johnny Churchill, had wanted her to flee to Canada with our youngest aunt, Frances. Winston had forbidden it, saying it would give propaganda to Goebbels, the Reich Master of Nazi Germany.

Penelope Tremayne, now Willis, also joined us. Her father was an Air Marshall and owned "The Lost Garden of Heligan" in Cornwall, now owned by Penelope's son, John Willis and let to Tim Smit with planning permission to restore the garden to the condition it would have been in 1849. My grandmother had been Penelope's godmother and my mother had written a book together with Penelope's elder sister, Damaris, in 1940, under the pseudonym Damiris Arklow. It was a novel set in Russia.

My mother's pet border collie, Pinkie, also came with us as well as my Exmoor pony, Butterfly. My mother also had two horses, Gaybird and Twinkle and we all went riding together plus the dog. We hunted with the Taunton Vale Hunt, me climbing over the jumps which were too big for me to ride over, whilst my mother led my pony across. I also had my dolls and their pram brought from Yester and so was very happy, apart from one thing. I missed our much loved Nanny, Nanny Baillie, who did not come with us.

CHAPTER 1
DONYATT

One day my mother took us for a walk down one of the country lanes over which spanned a railway bridge. As we got nearer, Hugo said, "Listen, I can hear a train coming".

My mother replied "Quick stand under the bridge and make a wish as the train runs overhead".

I shut my eyes and made the wish for my Nanny to come here. Once the train had gone, my mother suggested we went to the station. So on we walked and eventually reached it, where guess who we found waiting on the platform, case in hand, Nanny Baillie.

My father, David Morley-Fletcher, came by train to visit us at Donyatt, along with his dog Flame. The train

Nanny Baillie looking out of window at Donyatt

crashed but he and the dog escaped unhurt. In 1943, he had gone to Mussomeli in Sicily where he oversaw the daily management of sixteen townships, under the organisation of the Allied Military Government (AMG).

In 1945, he became Provincial Commissioner for the Allied Military Government in Bergamo. However, in 1946 he handed over the city to Italian control and moved to Venice, where he became Regional Director for AMG. His secretary there, Contessa Vanna Callegari Magrini, had been in the Italian Resistance during the war.

It was when he was in Sicily that he met Leila, daughter of General Petorelli Lalatta and had a son by her, Edwin, born in 1946. Leila wrote to my mother telling her that she had a son and that she should therefore divorce my father. My mother did so in 1946 when Hugo and I were made Wards of Court.

Daddy did not in fact marry Leila but moved to Germany in 1946, seconded by the British Army to the United Nations Refugee Relief Association, where he met and got engaged to Nora Vanda Lossman, daughter of Major General Arthur Lossman. He had fought in the Tsarist army in Mongolia during the Russo-Japanese War and in the First World War and in the Estonian Army in the Estonian War of Independence 1918-1919.

Major General Lossman was married to Maria, who was Polish and came from the part of Poland which is now Belarus. They had an estate near Tallinn which they farmed and Aunt Nora had been at Applied Art School in Tallinn. However, in 1941, the Lossmans, including Aunt Nora, were put on the Black Communist List to be deported to Siberia. They escaped by chance being put on trains, because they were in different places that night from normal, having gone into hiding separately. They only met up a few months later when it was safe to do so. In 1944, they escaped, first to Austria and then to Germany at the end of the war. All they had were some pictures wrapped in carpets, their silver and some clothes.

In 1947, Daddy having married Aunt Nora, returned to Britain where they lived in the Old Ship House, Henley-on-Thames. Daddy was in charge of the Administrative Staff College (a business school). Hugo, Nanny and I went to stay there for a holiday in the Autumn of 1947. Daddy and Aunt Nora and two other families had formed a pig club to supplement rations and the pig lived in the garden. I christened it "Aunt Nora", meaning it as a compliment.

In 1948, Aunt Nora was accepted for a job on the organising committee of the 1948 Olympic Games. It was run on a shoe string and Aunt Nora was horrified to be asked to be Head of the Information Bureau because she was a foreigner and did not know London but she accepted it, aged 26 years old and despite having only one week to prepare before the athletes arrived. In September 1948, Daddy and Aunt Nora went out to Nigeria where Daddy was Regional Director of West Africa for the Colonial Development Corporation (CDC).

In the meantime, at Donyatt, Hugo and I attended the local school - Jordans. To get to it we had to walk beside the railway to Ilminster each day. We had been told we must never cross the line, but one day we did, little knowing that the station master had been asked to keep an eye on us and we were in great trouble when we got home. It was not Hugo's first school as he had been to Yester Primary School when we lived in Yester House, where he was proud to have gone to the same school as the champion bowler to be, Willie Wood.

He liked Jordans, but I did not and had nightmares of the teachers being wolves and eating us pupils in turn, after playing a game like "the farmer's in his den". I was also sick after eating "yellow peas" for dinner. The only other thing I can remember about it is having to stand on a chair and tell the whole class how many letters were in the alphabet, which I

Sally Churchill, Penelope, Mummy, Vicky and Hugo on ponies, Donyatt

had learned simply by counting the letters which were up on the wall. My plight became more miserable in the Autumn of 1948 when Hugo went to St George's prep school in Windsor.

One night at Donyatt, I was woken by the sound of loud voices and lights in the sky and next morning was told there had been a fire at the battery where the chickens lived.

In 1949, my mother gave up farming and went to teach riding at Denford, a convent school for girls, near Hungerford, which was the junior school for a larger senior girls' school outside Chelmsford in Essex, where my mother hoped I would be happier. We took Butterfly and Gaybird with us but left Pinkie as there would be no work for her there and she was bad enough at Donyatt when bored, nipping the tyres of passing bicycles and rounding up lorries on the nearby road. She would stand in the middle of the road and lie down in front of them when she heard them putting on their brakes.

At Yester, my mother had once put her in a sheepdog trial. After her run, my mother asked one of the local shepherds what he thought of her? He replied, "if she belonged to anyone other than yourself, she might be running in the Olympics", meaning she was too petted for a working dog.

CHAPTER 2
RIDING AT DENFORD

The nuns at Denford were Canonesses of the Holy Sepulchre founded in 1642 in Liege as one of the oldest Catholic girls' schools. They fled to England in 1794 during the French Revolution and acquired New Hall in Essex in 1798 from John Luttrelle Olmius. They opened a Catholic girls' school there the following year starting with fifteen pupils. There they stayed and grew in numbers, until 1940. when they were told to evacuate to Newnham Paddox, between Rugby and Coventry, home of the Earl of Denby. Just in time, as New Hall, which was then used as an emergency hospital for the sick and elderly, was bombed in 1943, with considerable damage and a loss of seven of the patients, the number of dead later rising to fifteen.

When the war ended, the Earl of Denby gave the nuns a year's notice and it was decided to split the school of twenty two girls and start a new school at Goodings near Hungerford in Berkshire, with Mother Magdalene John as Superior. By 1949, there were fifty eight pupils with the senior girls returning to New Hall. In 1949, Sir Thomas Harrison Hughes, who was related to one of the nuns, gave Denford House to the nuns in memory of his wife who had just died, plus a generous endowment. The nuns then sold Goodings to Franciscan nuns from Taunton who had also fled from the low countries in 1794.

THE OTHER SIDE OF LIFE

Denford had one hundred and fifty acres of land, including stables and cottages, one of which we moved into. I started the school as a weekly boarder and my mother bought ponies, mainly from the New Forest, and set about breaking them in and teaching riding with the help of Monica, the girl groom, who lived with her parents in one of the other cottages.

Denford School with our ponies

My mother and I went on a course at a riding school run by a Mr Tate. Bracken, my favourite school pony, came with us and I rode him in the morning and a quieter grey pony belonging to the riding school in the afternoon. I was the only child amongst several adults there. On the first morning, I was put in the hands of the girl groom who got me to do easy things like trotting over poles on the ground whilst my mother and the other adults were schooled over an outdoor circuit with several jumps, including a horrid one half way down a hill.

After the first morning it was decided I was good enough to join the adults also because both of the ponies, especially Bracken, were good jumpers. However, we had to do difficult things like jumping whilst bending down and touching our toes and, worse still, jumping off our horses whilst they were cantering. I found this particularly difficult as it was hard to slow down my pony whilst I was running by its side to get on again. I also fell off jumping the poles half way down the hill but of course got on again as I was unhurt and the ground was soft sand.

One morning I found myself sitting on Bracken, crying as I had a headache. I asked my mother what had happened and she said I had fallen off Bracken when he refused at a combination of poles and I must have hit my head and lost consciousness for a few minutes. Mr Tate called me into the centre and I sat still and watched the others jump a four foot hedge that I was usually expected to jump although I was afraid of it.

I realised my fall must have been quite serious as usually I was expected to do the same as the adults which I did as I was terrified of Mr Tate who stood no nonsense or excuses. After that, he put Bracken in a jumping lane with a line of poles and a whip behind him to see how high he could jump he bent his head and knees and went straight under them, but when cross poles were put beneath them, he jumped his height with ease.

Back at Denford, we hunted with the Craven Hunt and did Hunter trials at Hidden Cottage, home of Roger Gresham Cooke, who became MP for Twickenham from 1955 to 1970 and who had three children, Hereward, Gerald and Rosalie, who became friends of ours.

My mother also took me to Chippenham Horse Show where after jumping a practice jump, it was arranged I should jump a lady's rather large pony in one of the competitions. However, the pony was too much for me and when he refused at the first jump I fell off, much to my shame. I was cheered up by meeting Harry Llewellyn, father of Princess Margaret's friend, Roddy Llewellyn and his horse Foxhunter. Some years later we were to see him jump at the White City in London.

My mother never favoured me apart from the fact that I usually got to ride Bracken, who was fairly high spirited but my favourite pony. However, once my mother left, when we had a new riding mistress, I was spoiled and had the time of my life, including going on the back of a man's motorbike to search for some of the ponies which had escaped.

Both my mother and her friend Penelope bought Alsatian puppies from Elizabeth Moncrieff, who bred them for their friendliness. My mother's dog Zany was rather skittish and not very clever but totally placid. Unfortunately, Tzar, Penelope's dog had a strong guarding instinct and though obedience trained by Penelope, was a danger to anyone coming to our house. He bit a little girl who lived in the courtyard, whose brother threw stones at the dogs and horses. Then he bit the owner of the local hotel we often visited, completely unprovoked and off his own territory, after which, so as to avoid a police order to put him down, Penelope gave him to the RAF police where his guarding instinct could be used to the good.

I was given a Siamese cat who slept with me, until one night, as a punishment, I was not allowed to take her to bed with me as usual. This was very distressing for me as I could hear her yowling to be let in from outside. However, having spent one night out at large, she discovered the thrills of the night and never slept with me again.

My mother and Penelope had interesting friends who came to Denford at weekends. One was Jimmy Lynch, whom Penelope had met at Camberley and would take Penelope and my mother to the opera at Saddler's Wells or at Glynbourne. Once, when there was a county ball at a nearby hotel, to which a social-climbing mother with two very dull daughters insisted in joining their party. Jimmy pretended to be the Crown Prince of Montenegro and quite took them in. Penelope and my mother also wrote a deadpan letter to *The Times* on the number of angels needed to patrol the earth for silence at twenty to and twenty past the hour, and even managed to get a reply.

Another person who stayed for a while was Margaret Noyes, daughter of Alfred Noyes, the poet. It was at a dinner given by my mother for her that she met the now Lord Nolan and got engaged to him. It was through her and her brother Hugh Noyes, also a visitor, that my mother was later to become secretary to Alfred Noyes, whom we eventually went to live with on the Isle of Wight, after a brief time in London.

However, all was not well with me at school. Despite having worn glasses from an early age, because of a bilateral squint and longslght, it became clear that my poor vision was holding up my reading and writing skills and I needed to have my squints corrected. Also, I was constantly unwell with sore throats and chest infections and was not putting on weight as I should have been. So firstly, it was decided that I should have my tonsils out and, secondly, my squints corrected.

My mother, meaning it well, put me in a private nursing home for my tonsillectomy. However, it was a horrid place and I was put in a double room with an old lady who died in the night. I then got an infection and instead of being in for a few days, was kept in for two weeks with four hourly painful antibiotic injections into my bottom. The food was totally unsuitable for children, far less for after a throat operation and the nurses were unsympathetic. Also, in those days, parents were not encouraged to visit, so I was totally miserable. Eventually, the day came for me to leave and I got my revenge, or so I thought, by refusing the stew served up to me for my last meal.

Notwithstanding, when some months later I was told I was going into hospital to have my squints corrected, I lay on the floor and screamed. My mother had to practically drag me to St Bartholomew's in London. However, St Bartholomew's was a different venue, well used to looking after children, though there were no separate children's wards and I was the only child in the female ward that I was aware of.

My mother and I were met by a kindly nurse who suggested she took me to see the goldfish whilst my mother took my things up to the ward. So, off I went quite happily, whilst my mother, having dropped off my things, slipped quietly away. After seeing the fish, I was taken up to a wide open ward with several beds, each of which had its own radio and earphones for free. This was a novelty for me and I lay quite happily on my bed listening to songs such as *Black Eyed Suzie*, which I still remember to this day. I was also given a little nurse's apron to wear.

I cannot remember anything of the operation, except that I had both of my eyes bandaged for a week after each eye was done. All except one of the nurses was kind to me, as were the other patients in the ward. So the days passed quickly although again, my mother did not visit. When the day came for the bandages to be taken off and the stitches to be taken out, the Registrar, whom I liked very much, told me I had a fly in my eye and if I stood still, he would take it out for me. So I did and in a moment, all was done and I could go home. The only other thing I remember is getting flowers from my Aunt Ursula, Daddy's sister, but I did not know at the time who they were from as they arrived during the time my eyes were bandaged. Later on, I was to get into trouble from her for not writing and thanking her for them.

Once back at school I read avidly now that I could see properly. Both reading to oneself and out loud were encouraged. There was a small but good library in the hands of Sister Mary Peter, who guided me round the shelves and pointed out the books about travel, in particular, about Scotland and the novels of Violet Needham, which I greatly enjoyed.

However, I was still not getting on with my school work as I was bored, which meant I played around, disrupting the class until I was sent out of the room, with my desk, by the lay teacher of that particular year who could not control me. This suited me fine as I had my library book always in my desk, so it was no deterrent and consequently I was down at the bottom of the class.

THE OTHER SIDE OF LIFE

At the end of the year, I moved up with the rest of the form into Sister Mary Peter's class. She wondered why someone who read everything they could lay their hands on, including some adult books, which she got out of the teacher's cupboard for me, was so backward in their lessons. She soon found out but instead of putting me out of the class, sat on me firmly, threatening me with missing my riding, films or even going to bed, if I did not keep quiet and pay attention.

As she was an extremely good and enlightened teacher, I soon became interested, as we acted out "Elizabeth, Captive Princess" when doing the Tudors, and made little cardboard theatres with figures and scenes from history for example, Sir Walter Raleigh, putting his cloak down for Queen Elizabeth to walk on. She also noticed that I had difficulty in writing quickly and so taught me italic writing. Furthermore, she made me her library assistant and also taught me the recorder.

We became firm friends and even after I left Denford, she continued to write to me and be a mentor to me. I will always be grateful to her for her kindness and dedication and for giving me the gift of learning as I gradually moved up the class, where I stayed in the top three, including when I went to New Hall the following year. I also became assistant librarian there due to her influence.

We were taught singing and I learned the piano at Denford but I was far more interested in playing Scottish songs out of a book Nanny had given me in practice time, rather than a very boring Grade I and II music of the time. I did not get good reports and was not encouraged by my parents to continue once I went to New Hall where it was an "extra", a decision I have regretted for the rest of my life.

Nature study was also encouraged and we had our own gardens and I was allowed to collect furry caterpillars of either tiger moth or large white butterflies from the nettles. I kept them in glass boxes in a lobby of the assembly room. However, one day the lids must not have been put on properly as suddenly there were shouts of "Vicky your caterpillars!" as they were crawling all over the floor during morning assembly. They were not a great success, as they cannibalised each other until they ended up as one large chrysalis which finally split open but no live butterfly emerged.

The Summers in those days seem to have been hotter and drier than nowadays as when half the school got chickenpox we were divided into two, and half ate and played and had lessons at great tables outside whilst the others stayed inside all day.

THE OTHER SIDE OF LIFE

After seeing the film of *Robin Hood* we played endless games enacting it. We kept to the same main parts and I was always the wicked Sheriff of Nottingham while one of the girls, Mary Feigan, who had lovely long flowing hair, was Maid Marion, and another, Sylvia Benson, who had short black hair, was Robin Hood himself. And then, of course, there was Friar Tuck and all the other followers.

There were trees and bushes around the lawns, which were really out of bounds. Nevertheless, we made tree houses and dens. In particular, there was the small stone remains of an old crypt whose floor was about four foot below the ground. Naturally, I would go in and explore, but coming out with my weight on my flexed left knee I either tore my medial ligament or cartilage which was not only extremely painful but also swelled up quite alarmingly.

I had to confess to the kind nun who looked after the sick, and she fetched the doctor and my knee was bandaged up for quite a while in a pressure bandage. However, the damage was done and it never completely recovered so that my knee turned in slightly, especially when bent.

In later life, this was to affect both my skating and skiing, during which I frequently caught an edge and fell, sometimes down steep slopes, because of it. It also meant I carried all children and suitcases on my right side, thus straining my right hip and causing early osteoarthritis so that I had to have it replaced at the early age of forty nine years.

THE OTHER SIDE OF LIFE

CHAPTER 3
LONDON

There was an addition to our family on 5th October 1949 when my half-brother Alan was born to Aunt Nora and Daddy in Lagos, Nigeria. Alan was a very good baby, and traders from Northern Nigeria would come down and lay all their goods out and bargain for them with Aunt Nora and Daddy. One time, one of the traders, on seeing Alan, said he would take the baby in return for his goods. Obviously Aunt Nora declined and as a goodwill gesture, the trader gave Aunt Nora a crocodile skin bag he had been going to put the baby in. Years later, when Alan went to work in Australia, the bag was impounded at the airport because it was a real animal skin.

Daddy and his family moved to Lusaka in Northern Rhodesia, now Zambia, in 1950, where Daddy was appointed Regional Director for Central Africa for the Colonial Development Corporation (CDC). Because the Chairman of CDC, Lord Reith, argued with the Governor of Southern Rhodesia and Nyasaland, the only country where CDC was allowed to operate was Northern Rhodesia, where Daddy set up and ran the Chilanga Cement Factory.

In addition, he was Honorary French Consul, which upset the Colonial Governor General, when on the 14th July Daddy was given a larger French flag to fly than the Governor's Union Jack. During the Mao Mao troubles, a volunteer police reserve was formed of which Daddy was Commandant. Aunt Nora joined the police force too, but Daddy blocked all her promotions.

In 1955, they returned to London where Daddy leased a house in Connaught Square from the Church Commissioners. The house was tall and narrow with two main rooms on each of three floors and a flat above and one below in the basement with smaller rooms. At one time Hephzibah Menuhin, sister of Yehudi Menuhin, who visited from time to time, leased the top flat from Daddy but kept her grand piano in our drawing room.

One day when she was practising the *Emperor Concerto* for a concert, I was sitting listening and Alan, then a little boy, was playing with his cars on the floor when Daddy came in and said he hoped we were not making a noise and disturbing Hephzibah, to which Alan replied "Hephzibah likes noise"; luckily, Hephzibah did like children.

My mother, Hugo and I had left Denford and moved to London in 1951 to 151, Portland Road, Holland Park, where Mummy leased the top two floors of a house quite near Rillington Place, where the Christie murders took place. Mummy cooked in a restaurant called Aribica and also read books with regard to their suitability for condensing for *Readers' Digest*.

Hugo and Mummy were in London for Queen Elizabeth's coronation in 1953 and stayed in Bedford Gardens, home of the Stewart-Richardson's and watched it on their television before going out to Marble Arch to see the procession. I was sent out of London to spend the time with two spinster acquaintances of Mummy's who also had a television.

I was not happy in London, where one was not expected to walk on the grass or climb the trees and there was no riding or animals, although my Siamese cat had come with us (but not Hugo's Hornby trains nor meccano!). When Mummy was working, we were looked after by a French au pair girl, Anne-Marie, whom we teased unmercifully. Among other pranks, we would wait until she went out of the room and then say "Let's have a fight", so we would pretend to fight, shouting "pig, pig" in French at each other and she would rush back saying "You must not say that, it is a dreadful word", which of course we knew perfectly well and would burst out laughing.

The only good thing for me was being reunited with my first cousin, Frances Coleridge, daughter of Mummy's older sister, Aunt Georgina, and who was just younger than me and like a sister to me. She lived in 33 Peel Street, Kensington, where many of the houses had been built for the French nobility, fleeing from the French Revolution. One of my favourite occupations was going with Frances to the Portobello Road Market, where we both bought and started collecting miniature crest china which I still own today. We spent our time going to museums, playing tennis and Mummy took us to the cinema to see the film *Where No Vultures Fly,* my first adult film.

    The other great event was being taken to the White City to see Colonel Sir Harry LLewellen jumping the puissance event on his horse Foxhunter where the great wall would go up to six or seven foot high in the final jump off. Later in 1952, Harry Llewellen, was to win a Gold Medal on Foxhunter at the Helsinki Olympic Games. I also remember being given a real boomerang by a misguided aunt which we mistakenly threw, through the luckily open window of the house opposite, without doing anybody any harm.

THE OTHER SIDE OF LIFE

CHAPTER 4
HOLIDAY IN SCOTLAND

    I joined Daddy, Alan and Aunt Nora for a holiday in Scotland when Alan was six years old. Hugo was sent with Frances Coleridge to stay with our Great Aunt Clemy at The Moult, Salcombe-on-Sea, much to his chagrin as he was allegedly better behaved than me. Consequently, he taught the other children a skit on the song "Oh My Darling Clementine" amongst other things.

    We visited my father's Step Aunt, Kitty Atholl, "The Red Duchess" so called because of her support of the republican side in the Spanish Civil War. The Duchess of Atholl was the widow of the Eighth Duke of Atholl and was Member of Parliament for Kinross & West Perthshire from 1923 to 1938, and the first woman to serve in a Conservative government. She was a Justice of the Peace for Perthshire and Parliamentary Secretary to the Board of Education from November 1924 to November 1929 under the then Prime Minister Stanley Baldwin. This visit involved us having tea at Blair Castle and I well remember the gilded drawingroom chairs.

    We also stayed with my uncle, Brigadier Ian Stewart and Daddy's sister, Aunt Ursula and their daughter Cherry at Achnacone near Appin. Aunt Ursula was secretary to the Duchess of Atholl for some time. Uncle Ian, when eighteen, was the youngest officer in the army in 1914 in the Argyle and Southern Highlanders and the first British officer to land on French soil.

In the Second World War, he led the Argyle and Southern Highlanders during the retreat in Singapore in which they played a distinguished part as the rearguard before Singapore fell to the Japanese. Uncle Ian was taken off by plane to India because he was an expert in jungle warfare, but had to be arrested before he would go and leave his men who were either killed by the Japanese or ended up in Singapore's Changi Prison as prisoners of war.

The Appin Stewarts were out in the '45 Jacobite Rising and at Achnacone there was a secret room you entered through the back of a book case for fugitives from the Hanovarian soldiers. They are one of the very few families who knew the secret of who killed the Red Fox, Colin Campbell of Glenure in May 1752, for which James Stewart of the Glen was knowingly and wrongfully hung.

I remember that we sang "baa baa gold sheep" to keep Alan amused on the long car journeys because the rams up North were dyed yellow.

In 1954, Hugo was confirmed in St George's Chapel, Windsor. I can remember Mummy taking me to the ceremony where the head chorister, who had a particularly good treble voice, sang the solo piece to Attwood's *Come Holy Ghost*. It was quite beautiful. I have never forgotten it and at the age of sixty eight, our kind organist here in Holy Trinity, Haddington, let me sing the same part with our choir.

Hugo was Head Boy of St George's at the time and wore long trousers, although he was not particularly tall. However, his best friend, Francis Cowan, who would accompany us when Mummy visited St George's and took Hugo out to tea, was exceptionally tall but wore shorts as he was not even a prefect. The pair looked most odd so in the end, Francis was put into long trousers as a special case.

Francis became a famous cellist but sadly was killed in a car crash near Edrom, Berwickshire, where he lived. Later, Alan followed on at St George's after Hugo left, having won a scholarship to Stowe in June 1954. Alan became a chorister after taking singing lessons from his godmother, and I enjoyed going to Evensong there when Daddy and Aunt Nora took him out from school.

CHAPTER 5
ISLE OF WIGHT

In 1953, Mummy was offered a job as secretary to Alfred Noyes, the poet, who lived in a fairly large house "Lisle Combe", near Ventnor on the Isle of Wight. We took the train to Portsmouth and then got the ferry across to the island which I loved, although the seas could be rough and I remember, at least one time, when the waves crashed across the deck and we were confined below. I was, however, allowed to stand on the stairs and watch the storm in safety.

Lisle Combe had a huge garden with tropical plants such as palm trees and fig trees; a tennis court and a temple in which there was a ping pong table. Beyond that there was a field belonging to the Noyes', a path parallel to the cliff and then a steep drop down to a sandy beach known as "Battery Bay". This could be reached by another rough path.

Next to it was a more accessible shingle beach favoured by tourists but we had Battery mostly to ourselves. We spent a lot of our time down there but had been warned not to swim before lunch when there was no-one around as there was a strong undertow and when younger, Mr Noyes had been carried out to sea and only saved himself because the current had passed Ventnor Pier which he had been able to grab hold of and climb out of the water. Indeed, I was once pulled over when fetching a ball from the shallows.

Hugh, Alfred and Mrs Noyes, Lisle Combe

Lisle Combe was an ideal place for children. Not only were Mr and Mrs Noyes and their son, Hugh, kind to us. They treated us the same as their grandchildren, Nicholas, Richard and Timmy Grey, who came to stay in the holidays. There were also neighbouring children, Jean Twinning who lived next door and another girl Glenys plus the Ogilvie-Forbes family who lived a bit further away. They all joined us for games such as tennis and adventures, under the guidance of Brigadier Green, who was an ex-army man. Richard Grey later married Hilary, one of the Ogilvie-Forbes' children.

One day we walked to St Catherine's lighthouse which was about three miles away and from which one could see France. Another time, when I was ill in bed, Hugo walked some distance to a cliff where the face had been washed away by a recent storm to reveal a herd of fossilised dinosaurs, a bone of which he brought back for me. We also found some other fossils in a tip near the house. Sadly, when we finally left Lisle Combe, Mummy did not think my fossils were priority things to take with us so they were left behind.

The adults arranged events for us on birthdays and holidays and I can remember a treasure hunt with clues written by Alfred Noyes for all the children. We were divided into teams of three and one hidden clue led on to another. For example, "Go and visit your patron saint" meant St Lawrence's Well which was between Lisle Combe and the Twining's house. Although Hugo's team read it as the village of St Lawrence which was further away.

One evening when Mummy, Hugo and I were alone in the house with Alfred Noyes and his wife, he announced that he would recite his poem *The Highwayman*. He drew the curtains and turned off the lights and having set the scene, started off. "The wind was a torrent of darkness upon the gusty trees. The moon was a ghostly galleon tossed upon cloudy seas" and so on.

When he had finished I asked him if he could recite "*Don John of Austria*, or was it too long for him?" So he started off again but this time went on and on and on, never ending. After a while Mrs Noyes said "Darling, I think Hugo and Vicky have gone to sleep".

So he stopped and said "that was *Gray's Elegy*. I was insulted that Vicky thought *Don John* too long for me!"

Alfred Noyes' son Hugh was one day harrowing the field beyond the garden with a tractor. I asked if I could have a go. He kindly said I could, so I climbed into the driver's seat and set off. All was going well until I came to a slight incline and started up it.

For some reason, Hugh called me to stop, which I did but my short legs could not reach the brakes so the tractor slid slowly backwards down the hill over the harrow, forcing it into the ground, Hugh ran over and stopped it going any further and the only bad thing that resulted was that the chain connecting the harrow snapped when we tried to go forwards again. No health and safety then.

We had taken Zany, our alsation dog, with us. She was very placid, or so we thought, until one day screams were heard coming from the coal shed where a man was delivering coal and on investigation, Zany was found pinning him against the wall as she thought he was going to put the coal on top of a litter of puppies she had given birth to secretly in the shed.

Sadly, at the end of 1954, we had to leave Lisle Combe as there was no room for us since all the Noyes' grandchildren were coming at once to stay.

THE OTHER SIDE OF LIFE

Mummy, therefore, leased a flat in a large Georgian House, Padworth near Aldermaston in England.

CHAPTER 6
WALKING BULLS AND RIDING ARAB STALLIONS

Padworth was split up into several flats and owned by Elizabeth, Countess of Bandon, who lived in one of them with her daughters Jennifer and Frin (Frances Bernard). Several families lived in Padworth and the ones we were most involved with were two boys Tarquin and Piers de la Force, both younger than Hugo and I, and their mother Falaise.

The only thing I can remember about them though is that when Piers became ill. I, in a spirit of compassion, gave him my mint set of Coronation coins, much regretted later, when I realised how relatively valuable they were. There was also Penny, a girl just a bit younger than me, who had two ponies, one of which I was later to ride. Frin Bernard and Hugo were close friends and even more so in later years, when we were all students in London at the same time.

At Padworth, we had a first floor flat at one end of the house with a rickety wooden outside stair leading up to it. We had some bantam chickens in a coop and run at the foot of the stair and a kitten. On Hugo's fifteenth birthday Mummy got a small dog called Quigly, the first in line of a succession of Boston bull terriers. She grew up with and curled next to the kitten and they played together.

However, there was a stray cat who would come and try to get at our

THE OTHER SIDE OF LIFE

Padworth House

chickens and long before we heard it, Quigly would rush to the door barking, and if we let her out, would run down the steps and chase it away. She was very intelligent and a well- trained dog. She went with Mummy to school and sat in a basket in the corner of the classroom.

    Mummy once again worked at my old school, Denford, but this time teaching a class. However, by then I had moved up to the senior school, New Hall. Mummy also worked for a second hand bookseller and while doing so, bought up an old library of books, some of which were quite valuable. A few she sold to pay for the rest and I still have some to this day.

There was a lady farmer who had a large prize bull which was quite tame with females but hated men. Mummy took him for walks as he was docile unless he met a man when he would paw the ground, snort and threaten to charge. The farmer also had a fairly small Arab stallion, Elrich, which was kept in a shed. Mummy offered to exercise him too and having found him quite docile on the lunge tried riding him and found he was schooled, quiet and obedient, so she asked if Hugo and I could ride him, which we both did.

Penny, hearing I could ride, asked if I would help her as she wanted to take part in a show, not far away, but down the main road. She told me that her ponies were not that good in traffic, especially the grey I was to ride, which disliked buses. I confidently said I was sure I could manage and so on the day we set off together. All went well until we came to the main road, which was slippery tarmac and suddenly there was a bus coming straight for us. My horse stopped dead and began to rear up on her hind legs.

Luckily the bus driver, seeing the problem, drew into the bus stop, just in front of us and waited. I shouted to Penny to get off her pony and lead us past it as it was shying a bit too but not as badly as mine, which I was terrified was going to come down on the slippery road. This Penny did and we managed in the end to get past safely. I did not offer to ride the pony again and I cannot remember how we got them home.

There was also a market garden beside the house where Hugo worked regularly pricking out plants in the greenhouse for pocket money after which the owner took him to the local point-to-point, where he trebled his earnings. I had a try working in the greenhouse with him but was wearing a thick red jacket with my back to the sun which was streaming in through the glass and I began to feel sick and nauseous and went home to Mummy, who realised I had heat stroke. That was the last time I did it.

One day, we went to a Peter May and Eric Bedser Benefit Cricket match in Aldermaston, and they were having great fun playing the locals and hitting the balls right over the roof of the pavilion. I still have their autographs in one of my scrapbooks and it was a great introduction to cricket for me. I was later to enjoy watching cricket when I visited Hugo with Daddy at Stowe and later in London at Lords.

THE OTHER SIDE OF LIFE

CHAPTER 7
SCHOOL DAYS - NEW HALL

New Hall School

THE OTHER SIDE OF LIFE

By 1954, I had moved up to the Senior School, New Hall, near Chelmsford in Essex. New Hall Manor was first mentioned in 1062 when the Augustinian Canons of Waltham Abbey bought it from King Harold. It eventually passed to the Earl of Ormond's daughter, who married Sir William Boleyn, grandfather of Anne Boleyn who sold it to Henry VIII in 1516 and who stayed there in 1527. He rebuilt it in red brick and renamed it Beaulieu. Mary Tudor lived there for several years when out of favour as a young Princess.

Queen Elizabeth I granted the estate to Thomas Radcliffe, Third Earl of Sussex, in 1573. He rebuilt the north wing, which had been destroyed by fire in Henry VIII's time. He put Elizabeth's coat-of-arms above the main entrance, where it survives to this day. The palace was again partly demolished and rebuilt by John Olmuis, later first Lord Waltham in 1713, but the north wing was left untouched and forms the present house which was acquired in 1798 by the nuns who started the school there the following year.

In 1954, the school had over one hundred girls in it and was divided into three houses "Poles", "Mores" and "Fishers" led by prefects and the Head Girl whom we were very much in awe of. The houses all competed for good conduct or bad discipline marks. We studied for GCE, O and A Levels in all the usual basic subjects but were also taught netball, lacrosse and tennis, gymnastics, elocution, ballroom dancing and ballet, art and needlework and three of the pupils in my class, including myself, did fencing.

There was also a school choir taught by an ex-singer, Lesley Duff, who got us to sing and make a record of the *Messiah* but without the male voices. Also we did the *Stabart Marter*. One could also study the piano with Miss Kerslake but I did not do it in the Senior School, much to my later regret. We had Scottish dancing sometimes on rainy days instead of outdoor games and as a treat, now and again, gramophone records in the evening.

Our day at New Hall started at 7.00am for 7.35am Mass, three times in the week and also on Sunday mornings, for which we all wore white veils. This was followed by breakfast in the refectory where we sat at long tables of eight, with a Prefect or Senior at each table. In my first year, I sat next to the Head Girl, Elizabeth Stokes. Later, when she left school at 17 years, she entered the convent as a Novice.

The Housemistress, Sister Mary Dismas, also presided over the whole room, standing watching us for any misbehaviour, or anyone who did not finish their food such as the horrid boiled fish which we got on Fridays for lunch and which I hated. After breakfast we all partook in housework until 9.00am when we had assembly followed by lessons. At 11.00am we had a break when bread, marmite, jelly and condensed milk were provided. Then more lessons until lunchtime. After lunch we had some free time then extra curricula activities, including swimming lessons in the outdoor pool, after it was built and opened in 1958.

Next we had tea with home made bread spread with margarine and jam, prep for two hours, except for those learning the piano, who did half an hour piano practice. Class 1 were taken up to the Lady Chapel by Sister Mary Dismas, where, if we had been good, she would read to us for the last half hour books such as *The Happy Prince*, *The Blue Flower*, *The Emperor's Invisible Clothes* or the Mary Plain books. If we had behaved badly a talking to and sit in silence.

We then had supper followed by bed and prayers before lights out. There were two open dormitories for the juniors from which one progressed to a dormitory with cubicles around each bed then to smaller shared rooms and single rooms for the Prefects. Everyone was in bed by 9.00pm when Sister Mary Dismas and the Head Girl did their final round and locked up for the night.

On Saturdays we had prep in the morning then free afternoons when we played tennis or rounders or tended the gardens, which we had been allocated. In the Summer we might be taken swimming. Also the school would play lacrosse matches against other girls' schools in Essex, and sometimes we would have films like *Ivanhoe* or *Henry V*, and in the evening Scottish dancing to records.

After mass on Sundays we had letter writing and everyone was expected to write home to their parents, which was fine for me except that my mother very rarely wrote back unless she wished to tell me about some monumental event. In the afternoon a nun would take us for a walk down the Avenue and we would all compete with each other as to who walked closer to the nun, even when little, holding onto her apron. Madame, our keen French mistress, would also seek out two to three of the senior girls if she could find them to go on a walk with her for French conversation and instruction.

Once in a while, for a treat on Sunday evenings for the whole school we would all get ready and change for bed and would come down in our dressing gowns and sit on the steps down to the ambulacrum. We would then listen to records of light classical music such as Gounauds *Ave Maria* and *Oh for the Wings of a Dove* but also more popular secular music, in particular a take-off of *My Fair Lady* called "Echos of My Fair Lady" with each song written in the way a famous composer would have written it, for example, Mendelssohn's *Get me to the Church on Time*.

I managed to get the record on the internet after years of looking for it to find that even the British Library sound archives did not have it. Some of the other songs I have loved and remembered ever since and have even sung one or two in church choirs. Another one I especially remember is Kathleen Ferrier singing *What is Life Without You?* out of Euridice.

A different happy occasion was, I think, at the Easter half term when, instead of going home, we had a break from lessons. We divided into our three separate houses: Fishers, More and Pole, and each house competed in doing a tableau of a chosen subject. One year we at Fishers did a hospital scene featuring an operation, all dressed up in white sheets and masks and another time, the guillotine scene out of *A Tale of Two Cities*, with some of us crouching beneath the desks with only our severed heads showing. I was Madame Le Frage, sitting by the guillotine knitting with the hair of the corpses. We were also encouraged to read at all times and there was a good library. Sister Mary Peter had written from Denford asking if I could get the post of Assistant Librarian to Sister Mary Frances, the Librarian, which I did. Sadly, I never had the same good relationship with her as I did with Sister Mary Peter.

At the end of 1956, as I was one of the older girls and had been top of my class, I jumped class three and moved into class four which was larger and split into two for some subjects. The dividing factor being those who took Latin and those who did not, who then got extra tuition in the other subjects during the Latin period.

I studied Latin, though I was bad at the grammar but managed to pass my internal school exams by knowing my *Virgil* off by heart and hence its translation into English. However, in the end, I did not take it for GCE. Maths also was a problem for me and less so French, although class four were far better at it than the class I had come from. I did have to do extra study in science and where the syllabus for GCEs included the work done in class three.

In 1957, Flindy Atkinson, one of my best friends from class two became ill, went into Chelmsford Hospital and finally died of leukaemia. There was a full requiem mass for her at New Hall and she was buried in the Nun's Cemetery. I still have a letter from her father, Colonel Atkinson, who was in the British Forces in Germany at the time. It was a very sad time for all of us.

THE OTHER SIDE OF LIFE

In 1957, flu swept through the school and each morning we lined up to have our temperatures taken and to say if we had any symptoms. On one particular morning I had a bad headache but instead of saying so, stupidly said I was fine. However, the thermometer told the tale and I was packed off to bed in a cold single room, where I felt miserable and wished I had told them I had a headache because then I would have been given something for it and been given some attention. Some of the girls were quite seriously ill but in time we all recovered and went back to the normal school routine.

Another time that illness threatened was in 1958 when I was studying for my GCE's. It so happened that Hugo and I both went back to school on the same day. Mummy and I dropped Hugo off at his station where luckily, as it happens, he refused to kiss me goodbye in front of all his peers. We then went to Liverpool Street Station where I caught the school train to Chelmsford.

All went well until breakfast the next day when Sister Mary Dismas came over to me and advised that Hugo had mumps and I must go into quarantine. I was put in the school infirmary, a large room with several beds and a cupboard full of books by Donford Yates, Berry and Co and others together with my work books and files. I was in my element and read the books avidly but did do some work too. Everyone was scared of catching mumps so no-one came near me except Father Butler, a frail, retired, Jesuit missionary, who was the school chaplain.

He took me for walks up to the Nun's Cemetery and other places out of bounds and kept me amused by discussing my future when I was to enter the novitiate and eventually become Mother Superior and would be the first nun to fly in an aeroplane. I loved the times with him as I was fairly lonely. Madame, the French Teacher, had a go at teaching me by talking French to me through my upstairs window but it did not really work.

At half term in 1957, I went home for the weekend. I was really looking forward to it. Mummy said she had got a new pony for me to ride and someone special for me to meet. I wondered what she meant by that. She arrived in the old car but a man was driving it whom I had not seen before. It must have been the person she had written to me about. She had said he was good looking though I did not have much chance to see as I was told to jump in as we were late and off we went. I was really looking forward to seeing my dog Rettie and my new pony.

During the journey, I became frightened as the gentleman drove in the middle of the road. At last we were safely home and I had a chance to look at Mummy's special friend. He was elderly, tall and thin with fairish grey hair and smelled of horses. We went in and Mummy introduced me to him as Colonel Robin Stewart. She said lunch was not ready and would I go and feed the pony.

Robin said he would come with me. We walked to the stables without speaking and he watched as I got some hay and took it to the pony in its stall but did nothing to help. It was a small skewbald pony which could only just get its nose over the stable door but even so, it managed to bite me painfully in the chest as I pushed the hay towards it. I smacked it on the nose, checked it had enough water and back we went to the house without speaking or any sympathy for the bite.

I set the table for lunch which was steak and kidney pie, not one of my favourites, and then apple crumble followed by cheese. All done, no doubt, to impress Robin but Mummy could have made something special for me. She served him first and waited on him all the time. I felt as if I might as well not have come home. He had terrible table manners and had hairs on the back of his hands like a monkey. However, at least the conversation was about dogs and horses, though I did not get much chance to speak. Robin subsequently stayed overnight. I was glad when he left in the morning.

Some weeks later, back at school, I got a rare letter from my mother telling me she was going to marry Robin Stewart and had got engaged. She asked me not to tell anyone. I burst into tears and the Head Girl, whom I sat next to for meals, asked me what was the matter but I would not tell her. However, Sister Mary Dismas, who was in charge of the refectory, had also seen me crying and realising that I was really upset, called me to her room.

At first I would not tell her because Mummy had forbidden me to but she gently persuaded me and I told her I hated my stepfather to be. She said that was not right and I would not make things any easier and talked to me about it.

The next time I was called to her room was after I had taken my exams when Sister Mary Dismas told me that my father had stopped paying my fees and that I would have to leave at the end of the term. It was a great shock to me as I loved my school and presumed I would be staying on until the Sixth Form to take my A Levels, in the hope of going to university to take medicine.

CHAPTER 8
BLAINSLIE

That summer, we moved from Padworth to Middle Blainslie, near Lauder in Berwickshire in Scotland. My stepfather would not allow Hugo and I to call him Robin so we decided to call him "Fa". I refused to call him Daddy, as I already had one in David Morley Fletcher.

Fa brought his land rover and horse box down to Padworth and we piled as much furniture and books into it as possible, though we had to leave quite a lot of the books behind. We drove through the night, the others sleeping en route, but I could not. We arrived in Scotland early in the morning.

As we neared our destination, Hugo and I asked excitedly how large was the house? What was it like? Was it like any of the ones we passed until we were nearly there?

Eventually, after passing through Earlston, we turned left on the A68 and went for about two miles along a minor road, past Blainslie Village and then, in a dip, stood a white doll's house like farmhouse with a garden enclosed by a wall surrounding it. There was a large yard in front of it with a big barn on one side and a small cottage and farm buildings on the other. We had arrived.

Middle Blainslie was a two storey farmhouse which my stepfather had enlarged. It had a front door with windows from the sitting room on the

THE OTHER SIDE OF LIFE

Vicky, Frances Barnard and Henrietta March-Phillips with dog Rettie

right and the dining room on the left, looking over the garden. The sitting room was divided into two by an arch. The front half was lined with book cases, with an open fire, sofa and two armchairs. The back half had a piano against the wall on the left and Mummy's large desk, which Fa had taken over, on the right beneath a window looking over the garden wall to the farmyard. In the middle, inset into the wall was an Indian picture made of uncut rubies and other jewels.

Through a passage between the sittingroom and the stairs one came to the larder straight ahead and then, round to the left, the kitchen, which one could also access from the dining room. The kitchen opened onto the back door which had a small porch. In the kitchen against the wall was a large coal fire Aga. Against the other wall a sink, wooden cupboards and a large table in the middle of the room.

Upstairs there was a huge tiger skin on the wall, two bathrooms and four bedrooms, mine being far the smallest with a bed and a fitted hanging cupboard and my crest china cupboard on top of a chest of drawers, my bookcase and a desk in the window and a chair. There was no central heating. Hugo's room was considerably larger and warmer than mine as it had the hot water tank in a cupboard in it and later, central heating.

My parents' room had an electric fire built into the fire place. The fourth spare room had no heating at all but had room for two beds and a large built-in cupboard, chest of drawers and a bookcase. Later Mummy had a garden conservatory added to the dining room side of the house and a downstairs loo. There was also a small saddle room built into the wall of the house at the back.

THE OTHER SIDE OF LIFE

CHAPTER 9
DAY SCHOOL-DUNS

When my mother married my stepfather, Colonel Robin Stewart, my whole life changed. Not only did we move from an upstairs flat in a large house in England to a farmhouse in Scotland, I also moved from a private girls' boarding school in a convent to a larger new co-educational day high school in Duns, Berwickshire which had 650 pupils.

It was formally opened by the Earl of Home on 31 October 1958, after I joined it. I was fifteen at the time and had six GCE 'O' levels and was hoping to do 'A' levels and go to university. However, one could not do 'A' levels at Duns High School where the children studied for Lowers and Highers, nor could one do the same subjects such as both history and geography together, nor biology, which I was good at. We had to do Higher physics and chemistry instead, which I found more difficult and both Lower maths and French, the former of which was my worst subject and English higher which there was no problem with. Even so, it was going to be an uphill struggle.

The day started early in the morning when I got myself up and had a quick breakfast in the kitchen on my own, then went out to join a younger boy from the village to cycle two miles to the nearest town, Lauder, rain or snow, even when he fell into a snowdrift. There we caught the school bus which took us over the hill to Duns. One of the senior boys was in charge of us on the bus and there was never any trouble and the hour long journey passed uneventfully and we arrived before 9.00am in time for classes, except for once when we got stuck in the snow.

I got on reasonably well with the boys and girls though at first I was teased a bit because of my English accent. A group would back me up against the wall and say "Come on let's hear you talk posh". However, I treated it with a sense of humour and would reply "I can speak Scots too and would recite "A braw bricht moonlicht nicht ye ken" and all would laugh. However, I could never speak the word "schule" the same way as them, but I was soon generally accepted.

Discipline at the High School was not the same as at New Hall. At both schools we played up the French teachers, but at New Hall Sister Mary Dismas, the house mistress, knew it and by chance would walk down the corridor whilst we were having French and if there was a racket going on, or if worse still, one of us had been sent out of the room to stand in the corridor, we were for it. I can remember once the whole class having been made to miss a weekend's film and write out French verbs because of bad behaviour.

In contrast, in the French class in the High School the boys would tease the French mistress almost to the point of tears. Either the Rector, who was a very mild, kindly man, did nothing about it or was completely unaware of it. Discipline therefore depended on each individual teacher. For example, in the science class the teacher was a man who stood no nonsense and used the strap at the slightest hint of cheek so there was not a cheep from anyone but he was also a very good teacher.

One good thing at Duns was that they did athletics which at the time New Hall did not, and I took to the discus and came third in the schools sports. The boy who won it broke the record and was mentioned in the local newspaper, *The Southern Reporter*. A bystander congratulated me and her neighbour exclaimed that I had not thrown it but just chucked it!

I also enjoyed playing *Sheep May Safely Graze* on my recorder with the orchestra at the official opening of the new school, though in fact I was in the school choir.

However, after my internal school exam results at Duns, the Rector had a meeting with the science master and my parents and me and it was agreed that I was not going to manage to pass the necessary exams to get into university. He suggested I give up the idea of doing medicine and try for physiotherapy, which at that time, was not a university degree and my 'O' level results were all I needed.

THE OTHER SIDE OF LIFE

The daily routine in the holidays was fairly regimental. Mummy would get up at eight and go down and put the dogs out and feed the Aga and then cook the breakfast of porridge or eggs on toast, tea and coffee, which we had every day. She would then call Hugo or me, whoever's turn it was, to set the table. Once all was ready at 9.00am, Fa would come down in his pyjamas and read the papers whilst he ate. After breakfast, Hugo and I washed up the dinner dishes from the night before and also the breakfast ones unless there was a daily help living in the cottage, in which case she did it.

Mummy would then go out with her dog Quigly and feed the animals on the farm. We had in turn; chickens, rabbits for fur, Aylesbury ducks, also mushrooms and lastly, Welsh mountain ponies and a few sheep. The horses were fed earlier by Billy, the eldest boy in the cottage, but we refilled the hay nets as well before lunch.

Once Fa was dressed, he would get the horses ready while Mummy put the lunch in the slow oven. I was loaned a horse *Princess* by our tenant farmer, on condition that Mummy would teach his daughter to ride for the Common Riding, and we would go out riding over the roads and countryside for at least an hour.

Before I had a horse to ride, Hugo and I would play board games, card games or Mahjong in his room, or would find useful things to do outside. For instance, Hugo dug a pond in the clay for the ducks or he would mow the lawn or I would pick fruit or peas from the back garden for lunch or we would play with the dogs. When Mummy and Fa returned from riding, we would set the table for lunch whilst Fa fed the horses and then we had lunch at 1.00pm. It consisted of a main course, pudding, followed by cheese with cider, beer or lemonade to drink.

After lunch, we would do much the same as in the morning until teatime at 5.00pm when Mummy had to produce extremely thin buttered bread and home made jam, ginger or fruit cake and a sponge cake or small cakes from the travelling baker who came once a week. Once we had television, we had tea in the sitting room to watch Children's Hour, as in those days it consisted of good stories, like *Little Lord Fauntelroy*, in later years, we watched the news, during which we were not allowed to talk.

After tea, I fed the dogs whilst Fa had a siesta and Mummy checked the farm animals, and then we again filled the hay nets but then once Fa got up the horses were groomed, the stables were mucked out and the horses rugged ready for the night.

THE OTHER SIDE OF LIFE

Fa then had a bath and I was allowed to play the piano whilst Mummy got the dinner of soup, main course and savoury ready. Again we set the table in the dining room until we had a television, after which we had it on trays in the sitting room at 9.00pm. Afterwards, we all changed into clean clothes or housecoats. Following dinner Fa saw to the horses and Mummy and I bathed and went to bed with hot water bottles.

In the winter, we hunted and in the summer we went to horse shows. Mummy rode in one day events and after a few years raced her horse *Eye Spy* which Fa had given her. She came fourth in the Ladies Race at the Berwickshire point-to-point, among others, which Fa had given her as a wedding present. *Eye Spy* was an ex racehorse and was very difficult to ride, as she had been kicked in the face while racing previously so she had originally refused to race again and reared up on her hind legs if a horse overtook her when out hacking, or if she did not like the look of a jump. My horse, *Princess,* was, on the other hand, really quiet to ride. However, we had been told she did not jump but managed to school her over the few jumps we had in a field and she seemed quite willing.

Mummy racing Eye Spy

THE OTHER SIDE OF LIFE

One rather wet day we set off with the Lauderdale Hunt, our local hunt, on a day when the Huntsman was away and the Junior Huntsman was in charge of hounds. The hounds found a fox quickly and raced away, crossing the River Leader, near Thirlestane Castle, with the Huntsman nowhere in sight.

We were with the Master of the Lauderdale Hunt, Jean Burns, and saw a man and horse cross the Leader ahead of us and so followed suite but not at exactly the same place but at a different point. Little did we know that the side of the bank had been cut away to make a swimming pool for the inhabitants of Thirlestane Castle.

Fa and Jean led the way but their horses pecked, spilling them into the water. However, Mummy and I, being lighter, our horses just swam across with us on top of them and we crossed successfully. Fa and Jean then being soaked, turned their horses back up a less steep bank and went home.

Mummy and I continued and eventually caught up with hounds and the rest of the people on the top of a hill. However, I had managed to end up in a field on one side of a fence and Mummy on the other. There was a wooden bar on top of the fence, making it into a jump.

Mummy said "join me on my side and we will go home". I rode *Princess* at the bar but she tried to refuse and when I pushed her, caught her foot in the wire at the side and did a somersault, throwing me off, luckily clear of her. I lay on the ground stunned but not hurt waiting for Mummy to come up to me but she sat frozen on her horse. Another rider then dismounted and came and asked if I was all right?

I shook myself and said "yes" and got up and back on to *Princess*, who seemed OK too and we set off home with Mummy. When I remarked that she had not seemed bothered about me falling off, she said, "On the other hand I thought you were dead!"

By the time we got home we were soaked and cold too as it had been raining, as well as our swim in the river. Fa greeted us with a glass of cherry brandy and never was a drink more gratefully received. However, we had to dry and feed our horses before going into having a hot bath and change.

The next day, Mummy trotted Princess up to check she was unscathed, after her fall, and noticed she was not quite sound. We took her to the blacksmith to check and he told us she was fine. She had been like that ever since she had fallen at a jump with her owner, Mr Douglas. Hence his telling us that she could not jump.

Jean Burns was a very great friend of Fa's and Mummy's. She would have me to stay when my parents had a dinner party and did not want me in the house or later, for house parties at Cowdenknowes, her large house, near Earlston, which she had inherited from her aunt, Miss Hope. There she would have parties for her nephew Geoffrey and nieces Felicity and Delsey, and she invited other interesting young people like David Langley, who in 1977 was to be engineer on the replica of Darwin's ship the *Beagle*, which mimicked his voyage to the Galapagos Islands.

When I stayed with her alone, she would take me to sheep sales, Kelso Races and once to an antique sale, where I bought a box of crest china to add to my collection and a Landseer print, both of which I still have. We would ride up the Black Hill of Ercildoune where Thomas the Rhymer was said to have met the Queen of the Fairies.

Jean also had a whole set of Georgette Heyer romance novels which I read avidly. She later asked me to break in and ride a fell pony *Jorrocks*, which I did under Mummy's guidance and later rode at a Kelso Show fancy dress event as an Afghan warrior, my outfit having been loaned by Jean. *Jorrocks* was then successfully sold to Lord Joicey.

I won second prize another year at the Kelso Show riding side saddle on another of Mummy's horses. I was dressed up as Mary Queen of Scots in a yellow velvet dress, worn by my grandmother when she appeared as Mary Queen of Scots at the Craigmillar Pageant in 1927 in front of Queen Mary and George VI.

CHAPTER 10
GIRL GROOM

During one of my summer holidays I went to Thirlestane Castle as a girl groom to help a friend, Linda Bingham, look after the horses there belonging to the Countess of Lauderdale and which her Connelly-Carews grandchildren rode. Lady Lauderdale owned Thirlstane Castle in Lauder, and the family consisted of Patrick, the eldest grandson, then Diana, who was "coming out" and Gerald, known as "Bunny", who was one year older than me and Sally, who was the youngest. They all rode seriously, showing and jumping their horses weekly, especially Diana and Patrick, who would be in the future Irish Team for the 1968 Olympics. Sally also rode for Ireland in the junior European jumping at Hickstead. Gerald became an amateur national hunt rider.

There were five horses to look after between us; Patrick's brown horse, a nervy thoroughbred; Diana's show jumper *MacTag*, and a smaller chestnut pony, *Copper*; Bunny's grey pony and Sally's small show pony *Lucinda* who was also grey. Linda looked after Patrick's horse and the chestnut and *Lucinda* whilst I looked after *MacTag* and Bunny's grey pony.

Linda and I lived and ate in the castle with the family but got up early before breakfast to feed and water the horses and groom them so they were ready to be tacked up and ridden after breakfast when the Connelly

THE OTHER SIDE OF LIFE

Carews came to the stables to mount them and take them out for a ride.

Whilst they were out, we mucked out the stables until lunchtime. The afternoons we had off, and in the evenings we all changed for dinner and played cards and once roulette, which I had not played before. I had no money so borrowed from Lady Lauderdale. However, I had beginner's luck and won quite a bit but sadly had to return it all to her, including the profit I had made. The evenings were fun as there were also young men staying for dances which they went to as escorts for Diana, who was a debutante. Before we went to bed, the horses had to be fed, watered and rugged up again, especially the day before shows.

I went with the family to the Edinburgh Horse Show where Diana was jumping *MacTag* but sadly took the wrong course and was eliminated. However, Sally showed *Lucinda* and got first prize but *Lucinda* reared up in the parade at the sound of the bagpipes. Luckily Sally stayed on.

Whilst we were waiting between events Diana put me on *Copper* but he was very excited. Even at a walk he would not stop but just flexed his chin into his chest when I pulled on the reins. So I was told to get off, and that is the only trial of a ride I had the full time at Thirlestane.

As the main reason I was sent there was to get riding and horse management experience, I was not happy, especially as Linda was paid and I was not but we were treated the same. When it came time to go home from the show, *MacTag,* who was otherwise very quiet, refused to go into the horse box and it took several of us, and only after several tries, to get him in and safely home.

On the whole it was not a very positive experience as they were not satisfied with my work and I did not like Linda bossing me around. So after I went home, I was nicely surprised when Lady Lauderdale gave me a leaving present of thirty pounds to buy a good pair of nicely framed spectacles. I had not been wearing glasses at the time as a Bates teacher I had gone to had told me I did not need them, which in fact I did, as was shown when one day after grooming *MacTag*, Diana said I had not done his face properly and it was still dirty. I had thought it was fine.

Back to Blainslie, where Mummy bred Boston Bull Terriers and we went to many dog shows where she usually was placed if, in fact, she did not win. We also had a trip to Carlisle for Mummy to take part in a "Try for Ten" (Questions) which she won after going twice, as the first time they ran out of time.

One of the things I most enjoyed at Blainslie was the music parties we had around New Year. Fa would make mulled wine, and Mummy, Hugo and I, and anyone staying, would make mince pies and we would ask a few friends in, notably Jimmy and Cureen Fairbairn, old friends of Mummy's who lived nearby. Jimmy was an ex-cowboy and had acted as an extra on cowboy films. He was also a great guitar player; Our cousin, George Bennett, who played the classical guitar, joined in with Fa playing the piano and me the recorder. More usually, I would sing and everyone else joined in to Country & Western or Classical songs or skits such as one on the Lauderdale Hunt that Fa and Mummy made up to the tune of *Widdecombe Fair*.

Christmas was celebrated low key compared to previously when the family lived Yester. Fa did not believe in stockings nor did he give us presents. However, we would open any Christmas presents we had received through the post at breakfast. Funnily enough, one of my best presents would be from Fa's elder sister, Kit Russell, usually quite small but especially chosen, such as a tiny Venetian vase or glass scent bottle, as I collected miniature china and glass.

Then we would go to church in Melrose and would come home and then go over to my grandparents' large house in Gifford for a full Christmas lunch with turkey and all the trimmings, Christmas pudding with silver charms in it, followed by crackers. After lunch we would listen to the Queen's speech and stand to attention for *God Save the Queen*, before opening presents from the grandparents, their dogs and sometimes from other relatives staying. Then back home for a dinner of home grown duck.

The only other time we went to church was on Rememberance Sunday as Fa was a member of the Scottish British Legion, and maybe at Easter.

Fa and Mummy had a lot of friends living in the Borders and East Lothian, so we also went to many parties and dances, and to the Hunt Balls, especially around Christmas and New Year, when our cold and stark Land Rover came into its own on the cold wintry nights driving through the snow. One night I distinctly remember is when Fa and Mummy were going to the Buccleuch Hunt Ball which was a very smart affair and Mummy fell ill and persuaded Fa to take me instead.

Fa was wearing his pink hunting evening jacket and white tie and the ladies were in long dresses. I wore a long silver evening skirt and blue low cut top which Mummy had made for me. We only danced a few waltzes and quicksteps as my stepfather did not dance reels, unlike Mummy and I who loved them. I remember being very impressed because the Duke of Kent was there and could be seen on the dance floor, although I did not actually meet him.

THE OTHER SIDE OF LIFE

CHAPTER 11
HOLIDAYS IN THE LAKE DISTRICT

Fa's sister, Carol Graham Harrison, invited me to join her family for a holiday on Lake Conniston. The party consisted of Joanna, Jessica and Helena Quirk and their parents; the Morse family, Jonathan, Oliver and Annabelle and their parents, who stayed in the big house *Lake End*, and Carol's family consisting of Robert, Sarah, Catherine and Tina and their dog, Silkie, and me, who all stayed in a two storey cottage.

Jessica had a canoe and their family also had a rowing boat which we mostly used, and the Morse's had a sailing boat. We all spent the time messing about in the boats just like *Swallows and Amazons* in Arthur Ransome's books and playing on Wild Cat Island. However, we first had to swim the breadth of Lake Conniston before we were allowed in the boats to prove we were seaworthy.

It was a very hot summer and we had a marvellous time and got on well together. In fact, it was so hot, that the hotel on the far side of the lake ran out of water, though we were all right. We went for walks and climbed the hills around the lake for which we were issued with scout whistles in case we got lost or had an accident.

Carol was very easy going but still the chores had to be done and we took turns to do the washing up after meals. Quite a formidable job, usually

Mrs Morse. Mrs Quirk, Carol Graham-Harrison and children round boat

done with Carol. Then one day when it came to my turn, Carol did not appear so I rather miserably continued washing up on my own. When I had nearly finished, Carol suddenly appeared and said what a wonderful girl I was and she was so sorry to have left me on my own but Sarah had broken her leg playing piggy back knights and horses. Luckily, David Morse was a surgeon and so was able to set Sarah's leg straight away and he drove her to hospital the next day.

Another drama occurred on a different day when we went riding at a trekking place nearby. We had all mounted various ponies, according to our size and capabilities, when the girl in charge of the stables got kicked on the knee and was unable to mount and ride. She had been told I was an experienced rider so she very kindly let me ride her beautifully schooled horse and lead the ride with the parents walking beside the less experienced riders and ponies. All went well though I do not think we managed to go faster than a trot.

All in all, I had a marvellous time and later Sarah and Robert both came to stay at Blainslie and I also visited them later when in London. We remained friends from then on for life.

THE OTHER SIDE OF LIFE

CHAPTER 12
CONNAUGHT SQUARE

Uncle Edward, Aunt Elizabeth, Aunt Nora, Grandpa Lossman, Margaret Pinder, Daddy, Alan and Andrew Butler, Connaught Square

THE OTHER SIDE OF LIFE

In January 1959, Hugo left Scotland and went to Manchester where he worked in the Calico Printers Association Works producing cotton fabrics. In September 1959, he went to Trinity College, Cambridge where he read Classics and then Architecture and Fine Arts, and rowed in the third May boat for Trinity.

I followed suite in the Autumn of 1959 and went down to London to stay with my father, Aunt Nora and Alan. To begin with, I took a job as clerk in Gamages Store in London for three months until I was old enough to start as a physiotherapy student at the Prince of Wales School of Physiotherapy where I was accepted to start in 1960.

I worked in an office composed of women, mostly cockneys, and another young girl of my age. Our job was to open the mail and sort out the contents – mainly money for mail orders which was then added up on adding machines by one of the more senior ladies. As I had never done anything like this before I found it interesting and got on well with everyone, so much so, that one day I was allowed to use the adding machine myself.

All seemed to be going well until the head lady checked the results and found out that I had added up two days' takings together which apparently I should have kept separate except no-one had said. She was very cross but all the rest of the staff stuck up for me and said how was I to know as I had not been told? Needless to say, I was not allowed to use the machine again. When it eventually came time for me to leave and start at college, they gave me a lovely card and a record or two, one of which was the *007* music for the film of James Bond.

I lived on the top flat of Connaught Square in my father's house which consisted of two bedrooms, mine having a large double bed, a small bathroom and kitchen and a sitting room with a table, sofa bed and desk where I studied but also had friends to tea, drinks and dinner parties, although normally I ate downstairs with Daddy, Aunt Nora and Alan. Hugo also stayed in the flat in the Christmas holidays and summer sales, when he worked at Harrods. I can remember one Christmas when he gave me a particularly lovely deep red coral necklace with three rows of branching coral sticks.

Later I shared the flat with a very nice quiet and easy to get on with girl called Ann Broome, who in 1965 went as a missionary to Ethiopia to Addis Ababa where she had first helped at a small nursery school of thirteen children, 2 ½ to 5 years old and a youth centre teaching different nationalities, supervising their play and teaching the older ones reading and writing. She also taught young teenagers at Sunday School for the Sudan Interior Mission.

In 1967, after a break having her tonsils out, she worked under a new contract with Princess Sofia, daughter of Emperor Haile Salassie, teaching twenty two 4 to 5 year olds at the school which had grown to four classes and about 80 children plus a bible class. She also worked in a children's club on Saturdays with 15 children between the ages of 5 and 11, doing hand crafts and games until 1971 when she returned to England to do teacher training.

Daddy had been Secretary to the Lord Mayor of London, and I can remember going to the Mansion House and being allowed to hold the Mace and feel how heavy it was. Daddy then lost his job and became a consultant with Amalgamated Industrial Consultants. One of his friends who visited us was Kit Aston, a man of great integrity and kindness who had spent most of the war in a POW camp, the troop ship he had been on having been torpedoed. Whilst in the POW camp he educated himself through the Red Cross. Aunt Nora worked with the British Council for Aid to Refugees.

I became friendly with some of the young in Connaught Square and we used to sing madrigals in a nearby pub, and carols round the square at Christmas. One Christmas, when we wrote letters to each of the houses with our intention of singing to them, we received a reply from Paul Robeson, the great negro spiritual singer, who apparently rented one of the houses. He wrote that he would be away in America at the time with his family who he hoped would be doing the same thing and wished us luck.

My grandfather gave me a membership card for Grosvenor House swimming pool and I would take my friends there and then have them back to tea afterwards. We also went skating, for which my step grandmother, Marjory Tweeddale, gave me a really good pair of white leather skating boots.

I also joined a small Gilbert and Sullivan opera company - the Philbeach Society - and we put on a very amateurish production of *Utopia* in which I sang in the chorus. In the summer, the society went sailing on one of the member's boats and played trains on a miniature railway owned by another member.

One day my godfather, Lord Tweedsmuir, son of the author, John Buchan, came for a drink at Connaught Square. I had not met him before but at school had read his book *Hudson Bay Trade*r. He wrote this after joining the Hudson Bay Company at Cape Dorset in Baffin Land, having been invalided out to Canada in 1938, and having contracted amoebic dysentery in Africa, with six months to live. However, the drastic cold in Canada cured him.

I was fascinated by him and his stories about life out there on Baffin Island and when he offered to take me there after I had finished my training, I readily accepted it. Subsequently this was not to be due to failing my physiotherapy exams the first time and also his friends crashing his ice plane.

When we moved to Blainslie from Padworth, we had not managed to fit all our books into the horse box so later I decided to travel to Reading by train to pick them up. I got to the station and went through the ticket office and got on the only train sitting on the platform. I settled down happily with a book once the train set off until the guard arrived to check our tickets.

He looked at mine and said "you have got on the wrong train, this is the non-stop to Newport, it does not stop at Reading!".

I was horrified and asked what I could do? He advised me that the train did go through Reading and suggested he threw out a bottle with a request to stop the train when it passed a signal box. I waited patiently till he did as he said but the train passed through Reading without stopping:

I was on my way to Wales and the worst thing was that I did not know how I would get back. Eventually we arrived in Newport and the guard marched me up to the stationmaster and told my story. The stationmaster took me to a seat on the platform and told me to sit there and not to move, and when the next train to Reading arrived he would put me on it personally. Luckily it was not too long before the train came and I finally got to Reading and I got a taxi to my old home at Padworth where I had meant to arrive about midday. Now I would have to spend the night with my old neighbours as it was too late to catch a train back to London and Connaught Square!

CHAPTER 13
CAUGHT BY THE TIDE

In February 1960, Penelope Tremayne married Anthony Willis at St Mary's Roman Catholic Abbey in Bodmin. She had met Tony in Cyprus, where he was working for the British Government Information Service and she for the Red Cross, during the Cypriot struggle for independence 1957-1959 under Archbishop Makarios. Later in 1958 she had been sent back by the *Sunday Times* as special correspondent to report on the state of affairs in the island now that Archbishop Makarios was released from exile in the Seychelles. The Greek Nationalist Guerilla Organisation (EOKA) had declared a truce to hostilities between Turks, Greeks and the British.

Sometime later I went to stay with Penelope and Tony in their lovely house *Sconhoe*, near Pentewan in Cornwall. One day we walked to the nearest village to look around the shops, after which Tony asked if we should walk back by the sea or over the quicker cliff top path. Penelope said the latter as it was nearly lunchtime.

After lunch Tony had a siesta and Penelope asked what I would like to do. I said that I would actually like to go for a walk on the sea shore over the rocks. Off we set, me in a smart summer dress and walking shoes. After about half an hour we came to a place where the path went steeply up the cliff face and we decided we had had enough and would set back home.

However, we had not noticed the tide coming in right up to the cliff face and the sand and rocks we had been walking on were now well under water.

We started back, toes on the rocks and gaps in the cliff face with fingers desperately clinging on to cracks above. It was at this point that I remembered that Penelope was a mountaineer and had been the first woman to climb many mountains in Cyprus. However, I was most certainly not and moreover was certainly not dressed for it.

Eventually we came to a bend in the cliff where the water was deeper. We were well out of our depth and there was no choice but to swim for it, suitable clothes or not. Luckily it was not long before we reached the sand and sighing with relief, were able to walk safely again, though now soaked from head to foot.

It was at this point that Tony appeared, coming out to find what had happened to us and he remarked that we looked a bit wet! Then he realised how wet we really were. After we told him what had happened, he swore he would never let us out on our own again and it remained a focal point for jokes for several years.

Penelope also took me for lunch with Lieutenant Colonel Desmond Fortescue who showed us round his deserted magnificent family house *Boconnoc*. The present house was built by Thomas Pitt, whose grandson became Prime Minister and a later Pitt had made further alterations. A previous house was mentioned in the Doomsday Book.

When I saw it there were large pictures hanging in otherwise completely empty rooms, which also had beautiful plasterwork. The huge ground floor windows of the three storey house looked out onto a park with magnificent trees, azaleas; rhododendrons and hanging roses. Desmond no longer lived in the house but instead occupied a smaller house built in the grounds which the factor had previously lived in. All the house was used for then was for period television productions.

One time when I stayed with Penelope I took a metal detector and using it on a grassy bit on the side of the road to their house got a positive response to iron. Eagerly I dug up the turf and found a whole lot of farm equipment, plough shears, chains and a gin trap.

CHAPTER 14
STUDENT YEARS

In 1960, I started as a physiotherapy student at the Prince of Wales School of Physiotherapy in Chepstow Villas near Notting Hill Gate, London. It was a detached house in a row of villas near Portobello Road, the famous antique, fruit and vegetable market, where we often shopped during lunchtime. The Prince of Wales Hospital itself was in a completely different location, where we went for our practical experience in our first term.

There were eighteen students in my year from diverse countries, ages, walks of life and politics. We all got on very well though an Irish friend of mine, Oonagh O'Donaghu, who was keen on nuclear disarmament and a socialist and I, a conservative, would have political sparring matches. Some students were straight out of school and some had previous working experience.

The head of the school was a large, amiable lady, Miss Farquharson. Beneath her were two student teachers; one, Mr Snooing, taught us physics straight from the book which he did not seem to prepare beforehand and who, Janet, one of the more senior girls, would frequently catch out when his diagrams did not work.

The other was a more diffident, but better prepared student of anatomy, whom the more worldly girls would tease. A Mr Cooper taught us physiology and would walk in and dictate our notes to us, commanding complete silence and attention. However, when one got home and tried to learn them, all was made clear. There were two other female teachers, one of whom taught us relaxation techniques and the other, Ms Tilly, Treatments later in the course.

We did six weeks of a practical nursing course in our first term. I did mine in the surgical ward of the Prince of Wales Hospital with another girl, Barbara Finlay. During the course we were sent to the operating theatre with patients from the ward. Barbara went first but fainted during the operation.

Mr Bannister with myself and fellow physiotherapy students

After that, it was my turn. I remember I was very nervous and apprehensive but was trying to watch what the surgeon was doing without being noticed. The operation was a Moors Arthroplasty or hip replacement. When the surgeon had completed the operation, he swung the patient's leg out to the side and looking straight at me said "that is so many degrees what do you think of that?"

I mumbled "good" and was glad to get away with it as I did not have a clue.

Later, when several of us were at Paddington General, one of the physiotherapists, Mr Bannister, who did the ulcers in the Outpatients and did not think we were working nearly hard enough, would draw the skeleton with the muscles attached layer by layer for us at lunchtime. I am sure he was partly responsible for us passing our anatomy exams plus the fact that we attended dissections.

He told us we should be doing two hours study every night which I found difficult what with Alan wanting me to play with him, and Daddy wanting me to socialise "like a young lady" when I finished work. Mr Bannister and the Singhalese Superintendent had both been prisoners of war as medical orderlies during the construction of the Bridge over the River Kwai in Burma. Being prisoners of war seemed to either make or break people as they learned what really mattered in life. We were a fairly unruly bunch of students and I can remember us getting a lecture from the Superintendent on our behaviour and manners. His were impeccable.

THE OTHER SIDE OF LIFE

CHAPTER 15
CAMBRIDGE

Mummy, Hugo and Fa at Cambridge

THE OTHER SIDE OF LIFE

In June 1960, Daddy took Aunt Nora, Alan and me to Cambridge to watch Hugo row in the May Bump Races for First and Third Trinity. He was number two in the boat in the third division. David Guinness who was also in the same boat with him in 1961, when they failed to bump, was later to share a flat with Hugo in London.

He became a great friend of us all. I cannot remember who won the 1960 race but it was always a great day out. We would go first to have lunch with Great Uncle Jim Butler, who was a history don at Trinity College and where you always got crème brullee for pudding, a speciality of the college. However, in 1961 we had, instead, a huge tea with Uncle Jim and later went to Ely, where among other old buildings, there is a magnificent cathedral.

One time, while we were waiting for the races to begin, twigs and small branches of trees began floating down the river from above us. As they were big enough to obstruct the boats, Daddy duly fished them out, one by one, but they kept coming down. So getting annoyed, Daddy walked up the bank to see where they were coming from, to find out. It was Alan who was having a lovely game putting them in and watching them sail down the river. We also attended the races in 1963 but by then Hugo had had glandular fever, which put an end to his actually taking part.

Daddy was also keen on cricket and would often take us to Lords Cricket Ground. We went to an Eton versus Harrow match on July 2, 1960, to watch Anthony Wagg, my step-grandmother's nephew play for Eton. This was always a dressy affair and one time Aunt Nora had put on a white dress with applique flowers on it which she had made from a pattern she found in a magazine when out in Africa.

She could not believe her eyes when she saw a woman walking towards her in exactly the same dress. After that, she gave it to me.

CHAPTER 16
THE ROYAL CALEDONIAN BALL

Back home at Blainslie in the Christmas holidays, I fell off Mummy's horse when riding alone in the countryside, to see if I would manage hunting her as Mummy had also injured herself. She bucked me off and I hit my hand on a stone and broke two bones in my hand. However, I managed to catch her and lead her home, despite my sore hand.

My stepfather took me to the doctor in Lauder who said I should go straight to the Peel Hospital, although it was already late in the afternoon. My stepfather drove me there immediately but we waited for hours before the Houseman came to see me as they were having their Christmas dinner.

He then sent me to x-ray where I waited again whilst the radiographer listened to the after dinner speeches. Eventually, I had my x-ray and went back to the young Houseman who confirmed I had broken two metacarpals and would need a plaster, though my hand was very swollen. This was completed and after asking for a sling, I went home with some painkillers to a very sleepless night.

A few days later, I returned to see the Consultant, without the sling, as my stepfather had encouraged me to use my hand and do my normal duties. However, the Consultant was not at all pleased because my hand was still swollen and he said the bones were displaced and I would need to have them re-set if not an open operation on my hand. I weakly said I was going back to London in a few days so perhaps it would be better to have it done there, which luckily he agreed to.

At that time, Henrietta March-Phillips, my stepfather's niece, was staying with us. She was the daughter of Gus March-Phillips, founder of the British Army Small Scale Raiding Force (SSRF), which was an elite group of paratroopers who undertook covert operations in Europe during the Second World War. Unfortunately, he was killed during the war aged only 34.

Henrietta's mother, Lady Marling, was holding a dance for her on Saturday January 7 down south, to which I had been asked. I went, despite my hand being in plaster, and danced but did not enjoy it as my partners kept holding my fingers. Lady Marling was very sympathetic and showed me to my bedroom where I promptly fell upstairs onto my broken hand. It was not a happy evening at all.

Once I was back at college, I showed my hand to Miss Farquharson who arranged an appointment for me with the Chief Orthopaedic Consultant at the Prince of Wales Hospital. He advised me that it was not a good idea to have open hand operations and that he would just re-set and re-plaster it. This he did and eventually it knitted together. I had the plaster off on January 26 though you can still see where the fracture had been to this day.

At the beginning of the year 1961 we had our in-house exams: theory, pathology, physiology, physics and anatomy which I passed. Then in October and November we had them for real including a vivavocca, anatomy and physiology exam, which I passed too, though it was interesting that the few students who had not studied physics at Higher or GCE level at school as I had, failed.

In April, my Aunt Georgina gave a cocktail party for my cousin Frances at Brown's Hotel, Albemarle Street, London to which I was invited. At that time she was going out with Gerald Gresham-Cooke. His elder brother, Hereward, was there so we re-met and became firm friends, approved of by both sets of my parents.

In February, Daddy and Aunt Nora said they would take me in a party, including Hereward, to the Royal Caledonian Ball at Grosvenor House, Park Lane which took place in May and that they would give me a white dress to wear to it as a birthday present. We went to Dickens and Jones and I chose a white satin strapless dress with a close fitting bodice and wide skirt. It fitted like a glove and so they bought it for me.

My first strapless dress! I was very pleased and looked on with great anticipation to the coming dance.

THE OTHER SIDE OF LIFE

Time passed until eventually about ten days before the dance, my stepmother said, "You have put on weight since your birthday. I think you had better make sure you can still get into your dress".

I got it out and tried it on. It was supposed to zip up the back but no way were the two sides of the zip going to meet, no matter how hard I held myself in. There was at least a three inch gap between the two sides and nothing to let out. I would have to lose weight and drastically.

I went on a strict slimmers diet of a thick pink liquid called Complan and two "Limits" biscuits taken three times a day instead of meals. As I was away from home for lunch I often ate nothing as I found the biscuits so tasteless, which added to the severity of the diet.

That same week Sir Simon Campbell-Orde, the organiser of the dance, rang my stepmother and asked did I know the Sixteensome Reel? She loyally replied in the affirmative. He said, "Good. Make sure she does, as she is to dance first lady in the Scots Guards."

This was to be in the Set Reels, with everybody watching, at the beginning of the ball as partner to Colonel Gregor McGregor of McGregor of the Scots Guards, whose wife was heavy with child.

When I came home that evening and my stepmother told me, I was horrified. I had never danced the Sixteensome in my life! And it was now imperative that I get into my white dress as nothing else would do. Aunt Nora rang Daddy, who was working in France that week and he told her to get sixteen people together for Saturday when he would be back and could teach me the dance. The ball was on the following Monday.

I still had to get permission from Miss Furquharson to have Monday afternoon off to practice marching into the ballroom in formation. However, when I stressed it was a Scottish charity, she agreed for me to go, provided the hospital, where I was doing my practical work, agreed too. Luckily they did.

On Saturday evening all went well and we made quite a reel party of it, except that in the middle of it there was a shriek of "The chickens!" from my cousin Cherry who was also taking a group to the ball and who had stayed too long dancing, leaving the chickens for Monday over-cooking in the oven.

Come Monday evening I ate nothing and my stepmother helped me to get into the dress. I held my breath and pulled my tummy in as much as I could. She pulled hard on the luckily strong zip and slowly, inch by inch, I was in but could not afford to laugh or hardly move.

When I arrived at the ball, my partner, Sir Gregor, lent over me and said "I hope you know this?" to which I replied faintly in the affirmative.

THE OTHER SIDE OF LIFE

I did not tell him that I had only learned it two nights before and that I dare not cough or laugh in case my dress split apart. In the end, all went well due to the miracle diet and I also did the Duke of Perth with him and his regiment, although most of the time I danced with Hereward.

I went to bed at 3.00am but got up just in time to be at college for our first lecture by one of the student teachers at 9.00am. I sat in the front row spreading out my hands on the desk and admiring my red painted nails, put on for the dance.

At break, Janet, one of the older girls, rushed up to me and said did I not realise that Miss Farquharson, who had come in to hear the student teacher, was sitting behind me taking notes. On her pad she had written "Miss Fletcher's nails!" in big letters.

Janet got some methylated spirits and helped me hurriedly take the varnish off and we went back for another lecture. At our lunch break I was called in to see Miss Farquharson. I went apprehensively into her office. She just glanced at my now clean nails and asked how the ball had gone. I told her about it and no more was said but the message was clear!

I danced in the Set Reels at the Royal Caledonian Ball again in 1962 but not with such a prestigious partner or set, and again in 1963 in a party which included Hereward, though I danced in the Set Reel with David Napier in the Second Highland Reel.

Caledonian Ball party with John Haynes, Penny Gilbey, Vicky, Roderick Grant, Katherine D'Ombraine, and Janet Morley-Fletcher

CHAPTER 17
BLAKENEY

Daddy included Hereward in a family lunch at his golf club at Denholm where there was a self-service buffet and you could serve yourself with as much as you liked. I dug in heartily and made a big meal of it. Hereward rang me a few days later to ask if I was I hungry because if I was not he would take me out to dinner but if I was hungry, he could not afford it!

He partnered me at various dances and in August took me to Blakeney in Norfolk, where his parents had a house, part of which they let, whilst keeping some rooms for themselves. On the Friday, we went to a dance and the party included his flatmates from London, Philip Wingfield and Peter Clifton-Brown and Peter's sister, Ursula, his brother Gerald and my cousin Frances.

On the Saturday, it was very windy, 26mph, so we were unable to sail but we played croquet and bathed and had a camp fire. Hereward took me to the butcher's shop and bought a joint of roast beef for lunch but I had to ask the butcher how to cook it as I had not done so before. We had rhubarb for pudding and Ursula helped me cook but, unfortunately, we put the plates beneath the gas burners on top of the oven and one or two partially cracked. Otherwise the day went well.

On Sunday morning we went to one of the lovely old Norfolk churches.

THE OTHER SIDE OF LIFE

Philip Wingfield, Hereward Gresham-Cooke and Vicky at Blakeney

In the afternoon. Philip and I sailed in Hereward's Swordfish with him. I had a lovely time as Philip was blamed for not helping me if there was anything I was having difficulty with. Even so, I managed to hit a wreck when having a turn at the helm, as I thought it was just a bit of floating wood. This I was not allowed to forget.

In October, Hereward had a cocktail party in his flat and I met a medical student, Roderick Grant, who took me home in his Mercedes. He loaned me his anatomy books and replica bones, and sometimes took me to his medical lectures. He also took me to films and out to dinner.

On 10 July 1962, Hereward took me to a British/American Ball at the Dorchester Hotel where the dance was interrupted at 1am so that we could watch the launch of the Telstar Communications Satellite on a Delta rocket from Cape Canarveral.

As I was at the age of "coming out", I went to several other dances, in particular, in parties arranged by a younger friend of Daddy's, Miss Margaret Pinder, who befriended me. In particular, she took me to the 500 Ball at

Claridges, with a relation of mine, David Starling. However, I sat next to a man at dinner whom I had not met before. We went through the tombola prizes and he bought several tickets and won, among other things, a lovely beauty case which he gave to me. Being fairly shy, after dinner, I fled back to David and do not even remember dancing with my kind benefactor. However, I still have the case to this day.

Margaret was quite a habitue of Claridges and one day when Daddy, Aunt Nora, Alan and I had helped her move from one flat to another, she took us to dinner at Claridges in our working clothes, much to the disdain of the waiters there. Margaret also took me to the Perth races and ball in Scotland with Lady Lucinda Mackay and her brother Lord Glenapp, and we stayed in a lovely house, Taymount, overlooking the River Tay.

At that time, several of my relations were getting married and a wedding I can remember in particular was that of Islay Campbell to Rohaise Anderson. Both were related distantly to my mother's side of the family.

The wedding was in St Mary's Episcopal Cathedral, Edinburgh on 22 July 1961 at 2.45pm. However, they only opened one side of the double doors for the queue waiting to enter so when the bride arrived on time, she could not enter and had to drive round Charlotte Square several times whilst poor Islay wondered what had happened to her and wondered if he had been jilted.

Rohaise had six little bridesmaids and six pages, dressed as heralds, and they all looked lovely. All was well in the end. In 1964, when he was only 29 years old, Rohaise's brother Douglas was to paint a splendid portrait of Her Majesty the Queen as Colonel in Chief of the Royal Scots Greys.

THE OTHER SIDE OF LIFE

CHAPTER 18
I LEARNED TO DRIVE

In October 1961, I arranged to have driving lessons in London but did not actually start until 4 December. I had two different driving instructors, one a petty small man whom I did not get on with, and one much nicer but very strict man who was an ex-racing car driver.

I can remember him pulling me into the side and making me change from 1st to 3rd gear again and again until I could do it without crashing the gears. I took my first test but failed because I turned into a side road so full of parked cars that I ended up on the wrong side of the road facing the oncoming traffic.

I had some more lessons and then took the test again. The driving instructor I liked least drove me to the test but on the way the gears of the car went so that in the test I had to double de-clutch every time I changed gear. I explained this to the instructor but I was a bundle of nerves and failed again. The racing driver instructor thought I should not have failed and gave me a test drive. At the end he said "Well Miss Fletcher you will almost most certainly fail again if you go on swearing at all the other drivers on the road!"

I took my driving test again accompanied by the other instructor and when we were sitting waiting for the examiner, he told me that the week before he had a pupil who could drive better than himself, failed by a certain examiner and that if I got this examiner, I would definitely fail.

In walked the man and he said, "That's him" as he came up and chose me.

I did my test starting off badly and then when it came to the three point turn, thought I had touched the kerb so put my hands in my lap and said "That's it!".

In an annoyed voice, the examiner said "Would you mind going on. I am taking this test".

At the end, he said to me, "You think you have failed don't you?"

I replied "Yes",

"Well I heard what the instructor said to you as I came in and you have passed!"

It nevertheless took me quite a while, under the instruction of Tim Robinson, another kind boyfriend, once I was back at Blainslie, before I could actually drive safely and confidently on my own.

CHAPTER 19
CALAMATIES

At the end of December 1962, Roderick Grant came to stay at Blainslie. There had been a lot of heavy snow so although we had a small party, only eight people arrived. The rest were snowed in. We made mulled wine and mince pies and played charades.

The next day Mummy and I went to a return party nearby, equipped with sacks and shovels, but got stuck in a snow drift, luckily within sight of the house. Roderick, Fa and Hugo saw us stop and managed to dig us out and after that everything went all right, although we returned home exhausted.

On the Wednesday, we tried to fetch our horse from a mile away up

Blainslie in the snow

the road but were stopped by snowdrifts as high as the wall on either side of the road but we were nevertheless able to go riding the next day.

On Friday 4 January 1963, Mummy, Roderick, Hugo and I went to the film *Hatari* in Edinburgh. Soutra was officially closed because of the snow but the garage in Lauder said that as we were in a landrover and had four wheel drive, we would get through all right.

This we did but coming back on Soutra in the dark, we came across a huge snowplough pulling a car towards us. The snowplough did not seem to see us and the towed car swung towards us as it passed. Roderick, who was driving, turned the landrover into the side of the road, where the snow was packed, to avoid being hit and there we were stuck while the men in the snowplough drove on oblivious to our plight. The men in our party got out and dug and we all pushed but the car would not budge. We sat there for at least an hour until eventually a smaller snowplough came along and pulled us out.

Roderick, Hugo and I had a train to catch that night from Melrose back to London, that is if it was running, as it had been stopped for eighteen days that year because of the snow. I packed hastily, hardly having time to eat dinner, and off we set once more, luckily with no more stops.

We caught the night train and settled down in a compartment to ourselves. In those days, as well as the sleepers, there were carriages with separate compartments with two long seats facing each other and racks for suitcases above and a door onto the passageway. Hugo was actually going to stay with Aunt Helen, who lived near Market Harborough and in his case were his best Christmas clothes; kilt; cufflinks; sporran and sgian dhub; and his Christmas presents.

For some unknown reason, he put his suitcase out in the passageway. We settled down to sleep, despite a lot of noise coming from drunk people in a compartment further down the passageway. At Carlisle, the train always had a long stop for the exchange of mail and there was a silence after the noise of the people getting off the train. Something made Roderick leap into the passageway. Too late. Hugo's case had gone.

That was not the end of our troubles. When we arrived in London, Roderick took me to his mother's house for breakfast. When I was doing my toilette, I put my hand up to my neck, where I had been wearing a pearl necklace, since the previous morning, only to find it was no longer there. However, since it could have come off in the cinema, in the snowdrift or in the train, there was no hope of finding it or any point in telling the police as it was not insured, I knew that my father would be furious.

After breakfast I had a sleep until lunch when Roderick took me to his flat and left me with his two flatmates. In the evening, we tried to go to the cinema but could not get in. We watched television until 11.30pm when Roderick took me back to his mother's house where I spent Sunday and went to church, before returning in the afternoon to Connaught Square for tea.

In February 1963, I celebrated my 21st birthday. I was working at Hammersmith Hospital on the day and when I came home to Connaught Square, Daddy and Aunt Nora were out, so I went down and watched an Italian film, *The Bicycle Thieves*, on television, which was very good. I then rang Roderick.

The next day, which was a Saturday, Daddy and Aunt Norah gave a wine and cheese party for me, to which forty five people, young and old, came and we danced reels in the drawing room from 9pm to 3am. I got thirty five presents, some of which, including a set of suitcases from Aunt Georgina and Uncle Arthur, I have to this day.

Daddy was in a jovial mood and he and Aunt Nora gave me a new double stringed set of pearls, to replace the set I had lost. Mrs Mould-Graham who at one time had been a girlfriend of Daddy's, before he met and married my mother, but who had married another suitor, gave me a diamond and sapphire ring, which Daddy had given her and which he had agreed for her to keep until he had a daughter who was twenty one.

This, for a while, was my most treasured possession but sadly was stolen from me later when I had a flat of my own in London, which I shared with Mrs Mould-Graham's daughter, Charlotte, and two other girls. Roderick gave me an art book on Botticelli which I still have.

I continued to do things together with Roderick, including going to the Reel Club Ball, in a party of friends in March 1963. The Ball was in Knebworth House, which was floodlit. I wore a blue velvet dress and my new pearls. Roderick wrote me a nice thank you letter commenting on how nice I looked in the dress and pearls. He also took me to the opera in April at Saddler's Wells to see *Cosi Van Tutti*. We also went to the May Ball at Cambridge, invited by Hugo.

However, on 3 May Roderick took me out to a Chinese dinner and told me he had fallen in love with Katherine D'Ombraine whom we both knew. Although he had been less affectionate lately, I was devastated at the news. I decided I would concentrate on my physiotherapy career.

On 10th July, I went with friends, including Roderick and Katherine, to a concert given by the Ariaga String Quartet. Roderick and Katherine took me home and told me they were becoming engaged. He also wrote to me saying he hoped in time I would be able to meet them both without any hurtful feelings and invited me to a cocktail party they were having for all their friends, although he said he would quite understand if I did not feel up to going. He also said he would like to take me and my mother, who was coming to London, out to dinner.

Roderick had a very good party the evening of his wedding to Katherine and I actually managed to enjoy myself. When in my bath, before getting dressed for it, I had my transistor wireless which Aunt Helen Berry had given me on in the bathroom, and was enjoying the luxury of it, when suddenly there was a news flash: "President Kennedy has been shot" and, twice again, "President Kennedy has been shot".

Gradually all the details came through but I was very shocked to hear one of the media ask Jackie, the President's wife, "how do you feel?" How would you feel when your husband has just been assassinated?! It was a shock to the whole World.

On Saturday, 23 November, I went to Roderick and Katherine's wedding at St James' Spanish Place. The bridesmaids wore red velvet dresses. I went in a group with Hugo and my friends and Gerald Gresham-Cooke, Hereward's brother, gave me a lift to the reception at the Landsdowne Club, where champagne flowed.

After a while, I did get over the hurt and Roderick, Katherine and I remained friends for years. Later, when working in Scotland and travelling down to mutual friends' weddings in London, I would join them at the reception. Also, years later, I went to stay with them at their house in the country, along with their children.

CHAPTER 20
HORSES AND COACHES

In April, I was asked by Lady Rhys-Williams to join a small party she was taking to see *The Mikado*. I was to go to her London house first for a light supper of smoked salmon sandwiches, to meet the rest of the party. I duly set off in plenty of time from Daddy's house but when I arrived at the Square, realised I did not know which house Lady Rhys-Williams lived in as I had forgotten to bring the address with the house number with me.

I walked round the Square looking at the few names beside the doors but theirs was not among them. Now in a panic, as it was getting late, I decided the only thing to do was to ring the bell of a random house and ask to look up Rhys-Williams in their London telephone directory and hope they were not ex-directory.

This I did and the people who answered the door were very kind once I explained my predicament and helped me look up and find the house number. I then walked to the right house and rang the bell, which was promptly answered, though I was told in no uncertain terms that I was late and they had finished eating and were getting ready to set out for the theatre right away.

Having been quickly introduced all round, including to a dark haired good looking young man, Walter Gilbey, we set off to the theatre where

THE OTHER SIDE OF LIFE

Walter, who was to sit next to me kindly bought me a box of chocolates to fill and cheer me up as I had had nothing to eat. In the interval, he and I got talking and we found we had a common interest in horses, as I liked riding. The Gilbeys had several coach and horses, which Walter liked to drive but he was not a very experienced rider, though at least one of the horses, *Shamrock*, could be ridden although pretty frisky.

We parted amicably and three weeks later Walter asked me to dinner at the "Beachcombers", a smart restaurant, to meet his guardian, as his father was dead, and to see a film. The evening went well, and a week later Walter drove me in a Brake in Regent's Park.

In May, he took me out again in the Brougham, in which we fetched, and I met, his mother. Later that month he took me reel dancing in his local church hall. Then the following week he came to dinner at Connaught Square and met Aunt Nora and Daddy, who approved of him, especially as he had beautiful manners, and we again went Scottish dancing.

From then on, Walter took me out fairly regularly for dinner or to go dancing or to go to events in the coach, including a traction engine rally. On one expedition he even let me hold the reins of the horses.

In June, I rode *Shamrock* in Regent's Park. This entailed getting up at 6.30am in my second hand Moss Bros smart hunting jacket and britches and boots and going to the Gilbey stables on the underground, amongst all the commuters. There my horse was brought out to me, already bridled and saddled, to the mounting block where I got on.

Accompanied by one of the grooms on another horse, we rode through the traffic, which I found quite daunting, to Regent's Park, where there was a special riding area. My horse was quite frisky but not as bad as the groom's horse which played up on the way home. Once back at Gilbey House, I joined Walter in the Directors' dining room for breakfast and then was driven by the chauffeur to college or to the hospital I was working in where I got changed. On one occasion, we picked up the Superintendent of St Anne's Hospital on the way. I did this several times, sometimes being accompanied by Walter on one of the other horses.

In the holidays in August, I went home to Blainslie. Walter came north too and we all went to the Edinburgh Horse Show. Mummy and Fa were in the Working Hunter's Class and Walter drove the coach with us on it plus some friends and my dog Rettie. When we came out of the show ring, we were stopped by a seething crowd of football fans who were rather menacing.

The coachman was alarmed and afraid one of the younger horses might become frightened and stand up in its traces and overturn the coach. So he whipped the horses up and drove the coach through the crowd. We got through safely, though it was a nasty moment. Another time, we took the Lord Provost of Edinburgh in the coach to a film and then to dinner in the Assembly Rooms.

Gilbey coach, Edinburgh Show

Mummy was worried about how much I was doing with Walter and advised me to make it clear that I was not hoping to marry him as I was still going out with Hereward. However, Walter and I parted on friendly terms and eventually, in Autumn 1963, he wrote to me and said he was engaged and in April the following year he married Jennifer Price at the Brompton Oratory in London.

I was asked to the wedding and remember it well. It was a wet blustery morning and Jennifer wore a beautifully simple satin dress with a train from the waist. The wind at one moment blasted the church door open and I was sorry for the little bridesmaids who must have been shivering in their shoes. It was a full Catholic service which was rather lovely, apart from the throaty choir. The reception afterwards was at the Hyde Park Hotel where the service was very bad but I enjoyed it as there were several other friends there too. Walter and Jennifer left the celebrations and were taken away by the brougham pulled by two of the Gilbey horses.

At 5.00pm the same day I went to the reception following the wedding of John Pinder, Margaret's brother, to Pauline Lewins at the Saddler's Hall, a lovely modern building. There were some very amusing speeches by John and the best man.

CHAPTER 21
ITALIAN HOLIDAY

In the holidays I either went abroad, benefiting from my student's pass or back to Blainslie to stay with my relations. In September 1962, I was invited to go to Rome to stay with an Italian colleague of Daddy's, Mr Mainardi, and his American wife, accompanied by Carey Liddon, daughter of another colleague, who was about the same age as me. We left for Rome by train in a couchette shared with a nurse from Westminster Hospital and two Italians. We went through Paris and saw Notre Dame Cathedral and the Eiffel Tower. We were horrified to also see animals in cages on the street.

We arrived in Rome in the afternoon. Italy was very dry from a seven month drought, like a desert. There had also been earthquake tremors too. I found the traffic terrifying when trying to cross the road. The welfare of the pedestrians was not considered. In the evening we went to the Colosseum and then had dinner out nearby with Mrs Mainardi.

In the morning, Mrs Mainardi woke us with cups of coffee and huge doughnuts. We then went to get our student cards and went to the Consulate and then to the Spanish Steps. After lunch, we visited the Pantheon but it was shut. Carey counted 50 stray cats of all shapes and size around it. Then in the evening we went to the church of Santa Maria Sopra Minevera, which had a beautiful mosaic ceiling and a Christ by Michaelangelo.

THE OTHER SIDE OF LIFE

The next day we went to the Vatican. It was magnificent, particularly the Sistine Chapel, which was almost devoid of people. I sent a post card to Mummy, Hereward and Daddy. In the evening we went to *La Boheme* at the magnificent outdoor stage at Caracalla. This was the ancient baths which was the summer home of the Rome Opera Company. It was, however, too large a setting for the attic scenes and as the seats were very expensive, we were sitting in the back so could not see or hear very well, though the singing was very good. It was also very hot – 92 degrees.

On Wednesday we visited the Villa Borghese. The interior was the best we had seen and I especially liked the Bernini sculptures. In the afternoon we managed to get into the Pantheon where Raphael was buried. Very impressive. We listened to the commentary through earphones. I bought a red straw sun hat for myself and a lipstick case for Aunt Nora. The following day we went to Ostia Antica, the ruined port of ancient Rome, which was much larger than I expected and had wonderful mosaic floors of sea horses.

We also visited Castello di Rocca, a real medieval castle, with holes for pouring boiling oil onto invaders. In the afternoon we sunbathed on the Lido. On Friday, we went to the national museum at the Diocletian Baths and to the Basilica St Maria Angeli. Then onto the forum and the Pallatine Hill.

The next day Mr Mainardi drove us to the catacombs of St Sebastian and St Callixtus, the latter most interesting. We saw a wedding in the church over the catacombs where a fabulous Agnus Dei was sung. In the evening Carey and I took Mrs Mainardi to the opera at The Eliseo, the small opera house. Because we were taking her, we bought front seats in the Circle which cost us less than the back seats at Caracalla. The opera was *Il Travatore* sung by the marvellous young tenor, Achille Braschi, who got three encores for one song. Everyone stood up and clapped, cheered and stamped their feet. It was most exhilarating. So when I got home I bought a record of the opera.

On Sunday morning we went to hear Pope John XXIII in St Peter's Square and then went to mass in Santa Maria Trastevere, one of Rome's oldest churches. There was yet another wedding, during which *Panis Angelicus* was sung. We looked at St Peter's, which was surrounded by scaffolding. Next day we visited the Forum and St Maria Nova, a beautiful tenth century church with a skeleton of St Francis in the crypt.

On Tuesday, we climbed up the cupola of St Peter's and visited its Treasury. On Wednesday, we went to the Castello St Angelo which had terrible prisons in one of which Dante's Beatrice died, and from the battlements of which Tosca jumps in the opera of the same name.

Vicky and Carey on St Peter's

We also dropped coins in the Trevi fountain at night. On our last day we went to Keats and Shelley's memorial house from which you can borrow a book. In the afternoon, we visited St Paul's Beyond the Walls and the Quirinale which had lovely ceilings and tapestries.

We returned to London via Switzerland and I fell in love with the Swiss Alps. The French President was on our train. On Saturday, we arrived back in London and Connaught Square. It was Aunt Nora's birthday so Daddy took us to the Dorchester Hotel for a dinner dance in the Terrace Room and I ate a very good scampi au gratin.

THE OTHER SIDE OF LIFE

CHAPTER 22
FRENCH HOLIDAY

In April 1963, Daddy and Aunt Nora took Alan and me on a trip to France in his old Jaguar. We left late but by driving fast, just managed to catch the boat.

It was raining in England but fine in France. We arrived at Calais at 6.30 pm and drove to St Valerie Sur Somme through lovely, unspoilt countryside with windmills and railway crossings. We had a good dinner at the Hotel de Colonne Bronze and then went to bed. We set out next morning at 8.30 am and drove to Rouen where there is a bronze statue of the Emperor Napoleon and we visited the Cathedral, which was bombed during the war but had been beautifully restored.

I had my first oysters in Rouen. Then on to Caen and Mont San Michelle where we arrived at 7.00 pm and to which we were able to drive up to as the tide was out. A magnificent place. We looked at the shops where the people were very keen to sell their goods. I bought a primitive mug and keyring and admired the floodlit rock. We enjoyed a good five course dinner, including clams and omelettes À La Madame Poulard, which we were shown how to cook. We got up at 6.30 am and visited the beautiful abbey and took many photos. After lunch of mussels and omelettes and ice cream, we drove to Dinan and onto Josselin, where Roland's Castle is, a toy fort indeed.

We then went to stay in Le Manoir Du Stang in the forest. We had a not particularly good dinner and then all the lights went out and we had to go to bed by candlelight.

The next morning was Easter Day so we went to church at Compere Cathedral, which was lovely and where they were having high mass. We then went to a castle and shops and bought presents. We returned to the Manoir for dinner and then went to a French party on a riverboat nearby, where there was dancing.

A beautiful young French girl came and asked Aunt Nora could she ask Daddy to dance to win a bet? Aunt Nora said "certainment!", and Daddy was as pleased as punch, having not been told it was only for a bet. We went back to the Manoir at 12.45 am to find ourselves locked out and we had to wake up the concierge to let us in. On Easter Monday the water supply ran out and it rained hard most of the day. We got up late and went for a walk in the woods, then had a quiet time reading.

On Tuesday, we left early for the Loire country. We stopped at San Nazaire to visit the mayor there who had been a leader of the resistance during the war and who was a friend of Daddy's colleague, Kit Aston. We had drinks with him and his family before going to a restaurant for lunch, after which he took us round the docks and showed us where the British ship, *HMS Campbelltown* had rammed the dry docks and blown up the German submarines. Years later, I worked in a Mission Hospital, where the Administrator had been the navigator on the same ship which brought the commandos who laid the explosives across the channel.

We left very late and drove to Chaumont via Nantes and Anges. Next day, we visited some chateaux on the Loire, some of which, like Blois, were sadly, completely empty and devoid of pictures or furniture. I thought a small moated one called Azay Le Rideau, would do me nicely!

We also visited Versailles. On Friday we arrived in Paris and camped in Daddy's AIC Office for the night. The next day I had lunch with my step great grandfather and his wife Mrs Einstein who I thought very sweet. They took me to La Bagatelle, a dear little house, which was built in two months for a bet. In the evening I went with Daddy and Aunt Nora to the Moccador to hear *La Veuve Joyeus,* which was good fun, although there was only one good singer.

On Monday, I went with Aunt Nora to get seats on the train home. We passed President de Gaulle's house. Never have I seen so many policemen

THE OTHER SIDE OF LIFE

in one small area. They were even on the rooftops. We returned with Aunt Nora and had a good crossing from Dunkirk and talked to two sailors and the Lieutenant until we left the harbour and stood on the bridge steps to watch the ferry enter the lock.

Azay le Rideau

THE OTHER SIDE OF LIFE

CHAPTER 23
COMING OUT

Whilst I was "Coming Out" and having a busy and exciting time, I was also working hard at college to get through my physiotherapy exams and to get experience in the five very different hospitals where we did our practical work. In 1960 and 1961, I had worked at the Prince of Wales Hospital and Paddington General, both general hospitals, where I first saw a baby being born.

In 1962, I was placed, much to my delight, at Great Ormond Street Hospital as I wanted to work with children when I qualified. In February, Prince Charles was admitted to the hospital and I was lucky enough to see the Queen when she visited. I was on my way out of the hospital to take a little Down Syndrome boy outside for a walk when she entered the main stairway, which I was about to descend.

In my time there I learned, among other things, the treatment of children with cystic fibrosis, which was to stand me in good stead in later years. I got on well there but did not stay as long as I wished as one of the other girls had not been happy in her placement at Camden Road Centre, a sports centre on our list. To my dismay, I was asked to swap with her which I did although it was not my cup of tea either.

In May I was sent to St Ann's, a small and very friendly hospital which specialised in children and polio cases. There were patients in iron lungs and other respirators and even a small hydrotherapy pool.

I got on well with the male superintendent there and was happy in my work. In October we had exams on the theory of movement and in November, our practical massage and movement exams, which I did not think went well and I also made a mess of the electrotherapy exam, which I heard later, I had failed plus the massage exam.

This meant I would have to resit my exams in the Spring and that I would temporarily lose my grant, which I was living on at the time, plus my father's allowance to Mummy for us, although part of that I gave to Aunt Nora for my keep.

I therefore had to earn some money somehow and I registered at Universal Aunts, a babysitting paid service. Babysitting for Universal Aunts was easy. I usually just had to play with the children whilst their parents were out; take them to the park or visit Hamleys and other toy shops to buy toys.

I had meals with them if they stayed in the hotel and put them to bed sometimes. I had two or three families whom I especially liked and worked for on several occasions. I enjoyed it and earned the extra funds I needed.

In November, I moved to Hammersmith Hospital, a very up-to-date general hospital which had a world wide reputation for kidney transplants and thoracic surgery and participated in a programme on television called *Your Life in Their Hands* introduced by my cousin, Dr Charles Fletcher, who was a consultant there.

The hospital was situated next to Wormwood Scrubs Prison. There I learned to do my first leg plaster of Paris and Bankarts bandages for a broken or dislocated shoulder. I was shown round the heart wards and recovery ward by Miss Hamilton, the Assistant Superintendent. I worked with her and also in the children's department where I was left in charge when Miss Stead, the children's physio was ill. In May 1963 I took my inter-retake exams, both electrical – where everything went wrong - and massage, which was not too bad.

I also attended outside lectures organised by the Chartered Society of Physiotherapists and went to lectures at St George's Hospital with Roderick, and in October had some private extra tuition from a physiotherapist, Mr Jenkins.

In November, I re-took the massage and electrotherapy exams. The massage was not too good, my nails were too long and later I was to hear that I failed it. The electrical exam was not too bad and the examiner was very nice.

THE OTHER SIDE OF LIFE

Afterwards, we went to a party, given by Margaret Pinder for her god daughter. Margaret's horse had won the 200 guineas race in France. In August 1963, my cousin Frances announced her engagement and in September asked me to be her bridesmaid at her forthcoming wedding. I accepted with alacrity.

One weekend Margaret came to Connaught Square and asked was I free to go to Paris with her as her horse *St Levantine* was running in a big race at Lauteuil Route des Lacs , and a friend who was meant to be going with her had pulled out at the last minute, so she had a spare plane ticket.

I was delighted and so off we set. However, the plane was late and we were in danger of missing the race. We hailed a taxi and Margaret explained the situation to the French taxi driver. He asked the name of the horse and when she told him, he got very excited and said he had bet on the horse, who was the favourite, and he would try his best to get us there on time.

He rolled down his window and waved and shouted to all the other cars to get out of the way and weaved in and out of the traffic at great speed. I thought my last hour had come but he did get us there on time!

It was very exciting going into the owners' enclosure to watch the race. However, *St Levantine* led all the way round the course until the last jump which she hit and although she did not fall, it put her off her stride and she ended up fourth. It was nevertheless a great experience.

Margaret Pinder was very feminine and always dressed beautifully, often in shades of pink and wherever she lived, the interior décor was always lovely. She was very kind to me.

THE OTHER SIDE OF LIFE

CHAPTER 24
PRINCESS MUSBAH

Another very feminine lady who was very kind to me in London was HRH Princess Musbah Haidar who had met my mother through Penelope and had been to stay at Blainslie when I was there.

She was the daughter of Amir Haidar, a senior descendent of the Prophet Mohammed and therefore one time Grand Sheriff of Mecca in 1916, who married an English girl, Miss Isobel Dunn, daughter of Mirali Colonel Dunn Bay.

Miss Dunn knew Prince Amir Haidar as she had been asked by him to supervise the English lessons of his young sons and to go out riding with them. She became a Muslim in order to marry Prince Ali Haidar and entered his harem in 1902 as Princess Fatma, at which time, he was living at Chamlujah Stamboul, a residential part of Istanbul, a virtual prisoner and exile in Turkey under the Turkish Sultan Abdul Hamid.

Musbah was born on 25 November 1908, the second child of Princess Fatma, after a difficult delivery, the doctor only having been allowed access to the room at the last minute. She grew up in the harem but was educated there, learning French, English, drawing and music lessons. This was not enough for her and, with the help of her mother, she persuaded her father to let her go to the English High School nearby but had to be escorted

THE OTHER SIDE OF LIFE

there and back daily.

In October, Ibin Saud entered Mecca and appointed Faisal as Amir of the Hedjez. He announced that all Hedjezis were free to return to their country but when Prince Ali Haidar set sail for Mecca, he was asked not to land and returned to Beruit where he had been living since 1926 and where his family joined him until his death in 1935.

When I met Princess Musbah, she was living in a flat at 25 Emperor's Gate, London with her English husband Major Francis Fripp. She was a great hostess and would ask me to lunch or dinner, sometimes alone, but often with five young princes about the same age as me.

One was Prince Ali, King Husein of Jordan's cousin, another was Prince Zaid who also came from Jordan, and both whom attended the Royal Military Academy at Sandhurst. There were also two Turkish Princes- Prince Omer Namak and Prince Osman Selaheddin Vassib.

Prince Osman was often accompanied by his Greek girlfriend Athena. Prince Osman was studying chartered accountancy and was the son of Prince Ali Vassib, Head of the Imperial House of Ottoman. Prince Ali Vassib

Princess Musbah and guests at Prince Osman's wedding

was exiled in 1924, and I had also met him at Musbah's. I remember him telling me that the Koran was similar to the Old Testament in the Bible.

Prince Osman was to marry Athena, daughter of Mr and Mrs Christoferides, in 1966. I can remember going to the reception after the wedding and being introduced to the ex-King of Bulgaria, an elderly man seated on a chair. I was not sure whether I should shake his hand or curtsey but before I had time to decide, he got up and kissed my hand, demonstrating the royals' impeccable manners.

The Prince I got to know best was Prince Omer Namak, also of the Turkish Royal family. He had been at school at Stowe with Hugo but had been brought up by Guardians as his father had died as a prisoner in Turkey.

The last of the princes was Egyptian, Prince Abbas Hilmi, born in 1941 in Cairo, and educated at Millfield School, then Christchurch Oxford. He worked as an insurance broker and in 1970 became the first foreign member of the London Stock Exchange. He was the son of Prince Muhammed Abdel Moneim who was arrested in 1957 and exiled, accused of taking part in an anti-Nasser plot.

At Musbah's, we would dine and play charades, consequences, and cards or they would tell my fortune: for example, who I was going to marry, by reading the coffee grounds remaining in my cup of Turkish coffee after I had drunk it.

Prince Ali and Zaid were different from the other three, who were quite Anglicised. Prince Ali was very independent, extremely patriotic and autocratic. Prince Zaid seemed just a boy beside him, aping his elder hero's ways.

Prince Omer came to parties at my father's house in Connaught Square and also went out with me to parties held by my friends. But going out with royals has its pitfalls.

One time when he went with me to a students' party, where there was dancing, someone turned out the lights for a short time. Omer was very shocked and complained to Musbah that I was not the nice girl she had told him I was.

She gave me a telling off and said I must be more circumspect where I took him!

Worse still, the same girl who had the party, asked would I bring Omer to dine with a Mohammedan Indian who had just arrived in London, whom she had been asked to entertain by the Consul.

Unfortunately, I became ill with flu that day so asked Omer would he mind going on his own. Reluctantly Omer agreed. I did not hear from him for a while afterwards but when I eventually next met up with him and enquired how it went, he asked what I thought she gave them to eat?

I said I had no idea and for him to tell me. He angrily replied "pork", which of course is banned by his religion.

CHAPTER 25
FRANCES' WEDDING

My Cousin Frances Coleridge got married to Neil Smith in St Columba's Church, Pont Street, London on Tuesday 7 April at 3.00pm, 1964. The minister officiating there was the Rev Bob Dollar, Minister of Dunfermline Abbey, a friend of my grandfather who was hereditary Chamberlain of Dunfermline Abbey, and who had christened most of us as babies at Yester House, Gifford, Scotland.

The afternoon preceding the wedding we had a rehearsal in the church at 3.00pm. Bob Dollar was in fine form but looking greyer and older than when we last saw him on holiday at Yester.

On being cautioned by Frances that I was standing a bit close to Neil, Bob replied, "I know Vicky perfectly well

Frances Smith

and have no intention of marrying her to Neil!"

However, everything went well except that my brother Hugo was ill in his bed, which was a blow to everyone as he was meant to be chief usher on the day. I visited him and stayed for supper, which I cooked for him and Peter Clifton-Brown and Philip Wingfield, his flatmates.

On the wedding day I had my hair done in the morning after which Mummy came and had lunch with me. Then I dressed and went by taxi to St Columba's where we got our blue and white headbands to match our long blue dresses. I was chief bridesmaid and there were three other older bridesmaids, including Priscilla Wrightson, Frances' best friend, and three little girls and a boy page. All the ushers were in a great fluster as Hugo, who knew almost all the guests, was still too unwell to attend.

Frances arrived pretty punctually in a beautiful satin dress with Granny Cameron's shawl and train. I felt very nervous proceeding up the aisle, and the bouquet I was holding shook when I stood in front. I nearly fell flat when Frances went to sign the register as she moved too fast for me to straighten the train. Bob Dollar was really good and made the service personal.

The reception was at the Dorchester Hotel, where we were photographed and shook hands for what seemed hours. When Neil was ready to go, I went upstairs to help Frances change but got lost in the hotel when sent down in advance and so actually missed the act of Frances leaving. She looked round to throw me the bouquet of flowers in vain.

So maybe that is why I never got married! Neil gave me a silver propelling pencil for being a bridesmaid, which I still have.

After the reception I went to our aged cousin Andrew Butler's painting exhibition and then onto the bridesmaids' party at The Savoy with Richard Hill who was best man and an exceptionally nice usher, Peter Kennedy Scott, who was a medic at St Batholomews' Hospital and two other ushers.

There was a very good cabaret with a James Bond act and a wonderful conjurer who produced about ten doves.

THE OTHER SIDE OF LIFE

CHAPTER 26
MUSIC

I continued to enjoy music, singing madrigals in a small group regularly and occasionally giving concerts. I was also lucky enough to go to my step aunt Kit and her husband Sheridan Russell's music parties from time to time.

Sheridan had learned the cello as a child plus the piano and flute. At age 14, he was in Monte Carlo when the 1914-1918 war broke out. Afterwards, he went to Italy and then on to London where he went to the Guildhall School of Music and started playing the cello seriously. He played in concerts in London, Monte Carlo, France and the United States. However, at the age of 35 years he realised he could not earn his living solely as a virtuoso cellist and needed to get an ordinary job.

He worked for various charities, in particular, The Hawksley Society for the Protection of Animals and Birds in Italy, becoming a vegetarian for life after seeing a cow slaughtered in Rome. In the Second World War, he joined the French Red Cross until Paris fell and then worked as a censor for Prisoners of War's letters. Eventually he was sent to Bletchley until 1943 when he volunteered to go to Malta under their auspices and from there to Italy with British Intelligence where he trained and sent out partisans.

At the end of the war Sheridan returned to Italy to go and tell the relatives of the agents who had worked for him what had happened to the men who mostly had been killed. On his return to Britain he did a special one year course to become a social worker at St Thomas' where he met Kit Stewart, my stepfather's sister, who was running the course and whom he was later to marry in 1957. His last practical placement was at the National Hospital for Nervous Diseases in Queen Square and having qualified on 5 April 1947, he got a job there and specialised on the problems arising from epilepsy.

When I first met Kit and Sheridan, they were living in an apartment in Lindsay House, Cheyne Walk, London, the house built in 1674 on the site of Sir Thomas More's garden. Their music parties consisted of gatherings of 30 to 40 people from all walks of life at which Sheridan and four musical friends would play unrehearsed music and then, in the middle, have an interval for drinks and small eats and time to meet and chat to the other guests. The whole evening ending by 11pm.

One time there I was talking to a Dr Bannister about hospitals and medicine when Kit, always the caring hostess, came up to us and asked me did I know who I was talking to?

I confirmed that it was Dr Bannister, to which she replied, yes but he is THE Dr Bannister, in other words, the person who had first run the four minute mile.

CHAPTER 27
LIVING WITH UNCLE ARTHUR AND AUNT GEORGINA

I continued to go on excursions with Hereward, including going sailing with him at Teddington, where there was no wind and, coupled with the fact that we had old sails on, made us last in the race.

I drove part of the way back to London and was, I think, more frightened than Hereward, who was wonderfully calm and helpful. However, in September 1964, Price Waterhouse, the firm for which he worked, sent him to America to work in their Boston office and after his contact with the Trinity Church there, he decided to enter the ministry.

Hugo, who was by then working in Christie's moved into Hereward's place, in his flat in Knightsbridge Court, London.

In June 1964, I heard I had passed my massage exam and took my final exams in July but was so nervous that I failed them. By then, Daddy and Aunt Nora had bought a new house with a large garden at Robin Hood Gate, Richmond. It was a regency house in bad repair with stables at the back which were let to a riding school and with a flat over the stables. We spent many weekends gardening there.

However, at a dinner in their house in Peel Street in September, Aunt Georgina and Uncle Arthur suggested I come and live with them, where there would be less demands on me than living with my father and I would

THE OTHER SIDE OF LIFE

Stag Lodge

have more time to study. A bedroom and a suite of rooms at the top of the house were available, Frances having moved out as she and Neil had a flat in Moscow Road.

After dinner Uncle Arthur put me on the train to Scotland to stay at Blainslie for the Lauderdale Hunt Ball at Thirlestane on Friday. On the following Monday, I went hunting on Jean Burns' pony *Candy*, after which I caught the night train back to London again, when I took part in a swimming gala after a day's work in the hospital. I finally moved in with Aunt Georgina and Uncle Arthur in October.

At Peel Street, I was free to study and come and go as long as I wished but joined Aunt Georgina and Uncle Arthur for all my meals downstairs and at weekends, except when I went to help Daddy and Aunt Nora at Stag Lodge, Robin Hood Gate.

Aunt Georgina was Director of Special Projects for IPC magazines and Director of *Country Life* Magazine. Uncle Arthur worked for *Reader's Digest*, so both needed an early breakfast like me during the week. It was a silent affair with Uncle Arthur reading the newspapers, though other meals were more congenial.

At the weekend, Aunt Georgina got up late and I would join her in her bedroom and would read her magazines and newspapers or just chat. Once up, she would watch the racing on television or play patience whilst Uncle Arthur spent time in his study.

I still went out quite often to Musbah's; Kit and Sheridan's; singing madrigals; or out with my friends and it was not long before Uncle Arthur took me aside and told me when I came back in the evening, I must be sure to lock and bolt the front door.

The next time I went out I returned about 10pm and took great care to lock every lock and bolt all the bolts and went to bed self-satisfied. I was just drifting off to sleep when I was roused by the frantic bell ringing and banging on the front door.

I thought whatever could it be and why did Aunt Georgina and Uncle Arthur not open the door? However, the banging continued and I suddenly remembered Aunt Georgina and Uncle Arthur had gone out that night and I realised with horror that I had locked them out! Furthermore, it was pouring with rain.

I rushed downstairs with great apologies but Uncle Arthur was not amused, though Aunt Georgina, who had a great sense of humour, just laughed it off.

THE OTHER SIDE OF LIFE

CHAPTER 28
I QUALIFY

At the beginning of 1964, I was working at St Ann's and the Superintendent, Mr Sitford, had said that when I qualified I could start work there as a basic grade physiotherapist if I liked, as they had a vacancy. However, when I failed he still gave me my own medical ward to work in directly under him. He helped me and did my work when I was at college.

However, Miss Morris at Hammersmith Hospital had also offered me a job with the children there in the Heart Team. The physiotherapists at Great Ormond Street had advised me to go to a big general hospital, like Hammersmith, for at least my first year, before specialising too much. However, I first had to qualify.

In October, I went with some of the other students to Clacton-on-Sea to see the Rehabilitation Centre there, the largest in the country. They had a self-contained flat for the patients to live in for their last week so as to help them to move towards rehabilitation into the community, which seemed a good idea.

It was a lovely day, though windy, so we paddled in the sea but we did not get back to college until 7.30pm. On another occasion, we visited Stoke Mandeville, the special rehabilitation centre for paraplegics. When we arrived we had a lecture on paraplegics with patients demonstrating

THE OTHER SIDE OF LIFE

movements which helped them overcome their physical disabilities. We also watched them swimming and saw a film of them doing their sports. I would have liked to have worked there for a short time.

On Tuesday, 24 November, I took my finals again.

The night before I was all ready to study into the wee small hours, but Uncle Arthur said that that would not help me. He explained that either I had done my work already, in which case I would pass, or I had not, in which case I might as well not bother going into the exam.

We agreed I had done my work and so he and Aunt Georgina took me out to dinner and regaled me with funny stories and practical jokes they had played on people in their younger days. On returning home I went straight to bed, then up ready for my exam at 9.15am the next day.

I went into the exam quite confidently and it seemed to go well and later I heard I had passed and got my certificate as a qualified member of the Chartered Society of Physiotherapists in December. What's more I had a job as Ms Morris at Hammersmith had kept her offer open, though I felt a bit mean to Mr Sitford who had been so kind to me at St Ann's.

I worked at Hammersmith for two years but subsequently moved back to Scotland as a result of my mother becoming unwell. I continued in my profession for a further 25 years until I retired.

THE OTHER SIDE OF LIFE